CW01303194

For the study and an understanding of esoteric knowledge as expressed most completely by Ibn ʻArabī, it is necessary to become acquainted with some of the terminology which he uses in his exposition of the way of the mystic in his esoteric advance.

THE TWENTY-NINE PAGES

An Introduction to
Ibn ʿArabī's Metaphysics of Unity

Extracts from
The Mystical Philosophy of Muhyid Din Ibnul Arabi
by A. E. Affifi

BESHARA PUBLICATIONS

Edited extracts from
The Mystical Philosophy of Muhyid Din Ibnul Arabi
by A.E. Affifi

This edition published by Beshara Publications
c/o Chisholme House
Roberton, nr Hawick
Roxburgh TD9 7PH
Scotland
1998

ISBN 0 904975 20 7

Printed in Great Britain

Introduction

Muḥyiddin Ibn ʿArabī, one of the greatest mystics of all time, was born in Murcia in 1165 of an ancient Arab family. His intellectual ability and spiritual aptitude were apparent from an early age, and he studied assiduously under many teachers in Andalusia and the Maghrib. After extensive travels in the Islamic world, he died at Damascus in 1240. He left more than 400 writings, in which the primordial principle of the Absolute Unity of Existence is expressed with unique clarity and fullness. To many he is known simply as *al-Shaykh al-Akbar* – 'the Greatest Teacher'.

The text of this book consists of edited highlights from A.E. Affifi's *The Mystical Philosophy of Muhyid Din Ibnul Arabi,* originally published by Cambridge University Press in 1938. The extracts presented here as a continuous text were first put together more than twenty years ago by Bulent Rauf, Consultant to the Beshara Trust until his death in 1987. His intention was to provide a complete introductory guide to the language and thought of Ibn ʿArabī, particularly those aspects of his doctrine which refer to the Unity of Being and the Perfectability of Man. It should be noted that Affifi's original work was in some respects not favourable to Ibn ʿArabī's point of view, though the author understood well enough what he was disagreeing with. Indeed, Affifi has done a great service by providing the raw material for what is perhaps the most lucid and thorough introduction to Ibn ʿArabī's metaphysics of perfection.

Long known simply as the *Twenty-Nine Pages* from the format of its original printing, this text has been a foundation for study at the Beshara School of Intensive Esoteric Education for many years, where it has been read prior to Ibn ʿArabī's own more demanding works such as the *Fuṣūṣ al-Ḥikam*. The clarity of the exposition and depth of meaning make it an invaluable reference work for all students of mysticism and the spiritual life, whatever their background. The only agreement required from the reader is to the premise that Reality is One. This accepted, Ibn ʿArabī's doctrine is shown, like all expressions of the highest wisdom, to be universal in its implications, and immediate in its address.

The *Twenty-Nine Pages* has been reprinted at least seven times for the use of the School, with minor editorial changes. This edition has been divided into sections to provide a better sense of the structure of Ibn ʿArabī's thought and to allow easier reference for the student. At the Beshara School it is always studied in groups, forming the focus for intensive discussion and acting as a mirror for the students' questions concerning their relationship with Reality. This is the first edition to be made available to the public, in the sincere hope that many will benefit from its grand yet essentially simple message.

Contents

Being	9
The One & the Many	11
Immanence & Transcendence	14
Causality	17
The Divine Names	21
The *A'yān al-thābita*	26
The Self-Revelations of the One	30
The Reality of Realities	33
The Perfect Man	35
Sainthood	41
Knowledge	43
The Heart	49
The Soul	52
Khayāl	56
Fanā' & *Baqā'*	60
Beliefs	64
Good & Evil	66
Love & Beauty	71
Index of Names & Arabic Terms	74

Being

Ibn ʿArabī's premise is the bird's-eye view – looking down upon a pyramid from above its apex, rather than viewing the pyramid from its base and looking up towards its apex. The apex of Ibn ʿArabī's thought is the point which is the 'Absolute Being'.

Ibn ʿArabī uses the term 'Absolute Being' *(al-wujūd al-muṭlaq)* or 'Entire Being' *(al-wujūd al-kulli)* to denote the Reality which is the essence of all that exists.

Reality is ultimately One, and Being (existence as a concept) is identical with the One Existing Reality which is the source of all that has existence. It follows that Absolute Existence, which cannot be anything but a 'universal concept', and 'Absolute Reality' *(al-ḥaqq al-muṭlaq)* are identical.

Reality (Being) is one and a unity, and Existence is one and a unity. Reality which is Absolute Being is actually one with Absolute Existence, though they may be separated in thought. Absolute Existence is the source of all limited existences. Ibn ʿArabī says, "Were it not for the permeation of God, by means of His form, in all existents, the world would have no existence; just as were it not for the intelligible universal realities, no predications (*aḥkām*) of external objects would be possible."

The real source of all beings is 'Absolute Being': a Reality or Being whose existence is identical with its Essence – a Being whose existence is necessary *(wājib al-wujūdi li dhātihi)*. This Essence is at once all the realised and the realisable quiddities *(māhiyyāt)* in the external world with all their properties and accidents, and upon this Essence, with its existence and manifestations, the human mind bases its notions of abstract existence.

Absolute Being, or Absolute Existence, or Absolute Reality, which is Entire, Indivisible, Universal and Infinite, is the Origin of all that follows.

Being becomes existent when particularised either as an internal mentation at the level of the Absolute Being, or as an extension of that being in the external manifestation. However, as we shall see, extension in this case is an extension without extension, although for our purposes the extension into manifestation is better considered as an existent in the world. Everything that has being may be said to have existence if manifested in one or other of what he calls *ʻawālim* (universes) or *marātib* (degrees) of being. The word *ʻalam* (universe) is often used in esoteric language to denote a global, unlimited, in-depth system.

As we will see elsewhere, there are considered to be 18,000 universes, though their number is infinite. This universe is both finite and infinite, immanential and spiritual, temporal and eternal, and above all, both existent and non-existent. It both exists in the knowledge of God as permanent and eternal, and in the phenomenal world as temporal and finite. What applies to the Universe also applies to Man. For instance, the Universe is sometimes called the Big Man, and Man is sometimes known as the small Universe.

Ibn ʻArabī uses the term 'not-being' to denote either:

1. things that do not exist in any of the universes or degrees of being – the pure non-existent *(al-ʻadam al-maḥḍ)*, about which nothing further can be said;
2. things that exist in one plane but not in another, under which we may class:
    a. things which exist only as ideas or concepts in a mind and cannot possibly exist in the external world;
    b. things which are possible or even probable existents, but which do not actually exist in the external world.

The 'pure not-being' can never itself be an object of our thought; other non-existents can and actually are. When we imagine we know a pure not-being, what we really know is its opposite (its logical contradictory), or the reason for its non-existence.

By a necessary being is meant a being whose existence is self-necessitated, i.e. it exists *per se*: and this is God alone. A possible (or contingent) being is that for whose existence there is no essential or necessary reason, i.e. its being or non-being are equally possible. An impossible being is one whose non-existence is necessitated by some formal reason. The philosophers deny the category of the contingent on the ground that all that exists is either necessary in itself or made necessary through another being whose existence is necessary in itself *(wājib al-wujūdi bi l-ghayr)*. However Ibn ʻArabī adds, "But the gnostic (*ʻārif*) admits contingency and knows its real place and what the contingent means and whence it is contingent, and the fact that it is essentially identical with *wājib al-wujūdi bi l-ghayr*." In fact, he emphatically denies the existence of the contingent *per se*, and admits only two categories: the necessary (as explained above) and the impossible.

The One & The Many

According to Ibn ʻArabī there is only one Reality in existence. This Reality we view from two different angles, now calling it *Ḥaqq* (the Real) when we regard it as the Essence of all phenomena, and now *Khalq* (the Immanence), when we regard it as the manifested phenomena of that Essence. *Ḥaqq* and *Khalq*, Reality and Appearance, the One and the Many, are only names for two subjective aspects of One Reality: it is a real unity but an empirical diversity. This Reality is God. "If you regard Him through Him", Ibn ʻArabī says, "then He regards Himself through Himself, which is the state of unity; but if you regard Him through yourself then the unity vanishes".

The One is everywhere as an Essence, and nowhere as the Universal Essence which is above and beyond all 'where' and 'how'. "Unity has no other meaning than two (or more) things being actually identical, but conceptually distinguishable the one from the other; so in one sense the one **is** the other; in another it is not." "Multiplicity is due to different points of view, not to an actual division in the One Essence (*'Ayn*)."

The whole of Ibn 'Arabī's metaphysics rests on this distinction and there is not a single point in his system where it is not introduced in some form or other.

Owing to our finite minds and our inability to grasp the Whole as a Whole, we regard it as a plurality of beings, ascribing to each one characteristics which distinguish it from the rest. Only a person possessed of the vision of a mystic, Ibn 'Arabī would say, can transcend, in a supra-mental state of intuition, all the multiplicity of forms and 'see' the reality that underlies them. What seem to multiply the One are the *aḥkām* (predications) which we predicate of external objects – the fact that we bring them under categories of colour, size, shape, and temporal and spatial relations, etc. In itself the One is simple and indivisible.

To express it in theological language, as Ibn 'Arabī sometimes does, the One is *al-Ḥaqq* (the Real or God), the Many are *al-Khalq* (created beings, phenomenal world); the One is the Lord, the Many are the servants; the One is a unity (*jam'*), the Many are a diversity (*farq*); and so on.

Now we are in a position to understand the apparent paradoxes in which Ibn 'Arabī often revels, such as "the creator is the created"; "I am He and He is I"; "I am He and not He"; "*Ḥaqq* is *Khalq* and *Khalq* is *Ḥaqq*"; "*Ḥaqq* is not *Khalq* and *Khalq* is not *Ḥaqq*"; and so on and so on. Explained on this relative notion of the two aspects of Reality, these paradoxes are no paradoxes at all. There is a complete reciprocity between the One and the Many as understood by Ibn 'Arabī, and complete mutual dependence. Like two logical correlatives, neither has any meaning without the other.

The relation between the One and the Many is often explained by Ibn ʿArabī by means of metaphors, and the utmost care should be taken in understanding them correctly.

The metaphor of the 'mirror' and 'images' is closely allied to that of the 'object' and its 'shadow'. The One is regarded as an object whose image is reflected in different mirrors; the images appearing in different forms and shapes according to the nature of each mirror (locus). The Many (phenomenal world) is the mirror-image, the shadow of the Real object beyond. The whole world is like a shadow play. "We are sufficiently far", he says, "from the screen on which the phenomenal objects are reflected to believe that what we see (on the screen) is all that is real." To rule out any implication of duality, he definitely states that the source of the shadow and the shadow itself are one.

The metaphor of 'permeation' and 'spiritual food': the Many permeates the One in the sense in which qualities, colour say, permeate substances. The One, on the other hand, permeates the Many as food permeates a body. God is our sustaining spiritual food because He is our essence. The phenomenal world is also His food because it is through it that God is endowed with Attributes *(aḥkām)*.

Ibn ʿArabī holds that the spiritual governs and controls the material everywhere: the One Universal Substance abides in all and governs all. "The Many are to the One like a vessel *(inā)* in which His Essence subsists." According to Ibn ʿArabī, spirit is 'materia' to matter. The whole Universe may be One Universal Spirit possessing even a higher degree of unity than that of a human mind. The ultimate solution of the problem rests with the supra-mental intuition of the mystic, which alone perceives the unity as a unity.

Ibn ʿArabī warns us that should we maintain a distinction between the Real and the Phenomenal (*Ḥaqq* and *Khalq*), thus explained as Essence and Form, or Reality and Appearance, etc., we should not, even on his doctrine, predicate of one what is predicable of the other, except in the strict sense of regarding them as ultimately and essentially One (*Ḥaqq*). The One Essence transcends all the forms and whatever characteristics belong to them.

Immanence & Transcendence

We have already seen that the duality of *Ḥaqq* and *Khalq* is not, in Ibn 'Arabī's view, a real duality of beings but a duality of what we might call differentiating aspects. Differentiating aspects are identified in his philosophy with what he calls transcendence and immanence (*tanzīh* and *tashbīh*). In Ibn 'Arabī's doctrine of transcendence and immanence, immanence is not understood to mean that God possesses hearing, or sight, or hands etc., but rather that He is immanent in all that hears and sees, and this constitutes His immanence (*tashbīh*). On the other hand, His Essence is not limited to one being or a group of beings that hear and see, but is manifested in all such beings whatever. In this sense God is transcendent because He is above all limitation and individualisation. As a universal substance, He is the Essence of all that is. Thus Ibn 'Arabī reduces *tanzīh* and *tashbīh* to absoluteness (*iṭlāq*) and limitedness (*taqyīd*).

Ibn 'Arabī emphatically denies anthropomorphism and corporealism, and the Christian doctrine of incarnation (*ḥulūl*). To say that Christ is God is true, he says, in the sense that everything else is God, and to say that Christ is the son of Mary is also true, but to say that God is Christ the son of Mary is false, because this would imply that He is Christ and nothing else. God is you and I and everything else in the universe. He is all that is perceptible and imperceptible; material or spiritual. It is infidelity (*kufr*) to say that He is you alone or I alone or Christ alone, or to limit Him in any form whatever, even in a conceptual form. When a man says that he has seen God in a dream with such and such a colour, size or form, all that he wishes to say is that God has revealed Himself to him in one of His infinite forms, for He reveals Himself in intelligible as well as in concrete forms. So what the man has really seen is a form of God, not God Himself.

Ibn ʿArabī holds that transcendence and immanence are two fundamental aspects of Reality as we know it. Neither of them would be sufficient without the other if we want to give a complete account of Reality. The *Ḥaqq* of whom transcendence is asserted is the same as the *Khalq* of whom immanence is asserted, although (logically) the Creator is distinguished from the created.

Although Ibn ʿArabī asserts that everything and all things are God (the immanent aspect), he takes care not to assert the converse. God is the Unity behind the multiplicity and the Reality behind the Appearance (the transcendent aspect). He says that it is not transcendence as asserted by man which explains the real nature of God as the Absolute. Even the most abstract transcendence (conceived by man) is a form of limitation, because it implies, at least, the existence of an asserter besides that of God. Further, to assert anything of anything is to limit it; therefore, the assertion even of absolute transcendence of God is a limitation. The assertion, made by the intellect, of the transcendence of God is only a convenient way of contrasting the two aspects of Reality as we understand it, but it does not explain its nature.

Tawḥīd (unification, union) belongs to the *Muwaḥḥid* (the Unifier), not to God, since God is above all assertions. No-one except God Himself knows His real transcendent aspect. The perfect Sufi, in his ecstatic flight, might have a glimpse of this unity, not through the intellect but by means of a supra-mental intuition which belongs only to such a state. This higher form of transcendence is independent of all assertion. It belongs to the Divine Essence *per se* and *a se*, and it is what

Ibn ʿArabī calls the transcendence of the unity (*tanzīh al-tawḥīd*). The absolute unity and simplicity of the Divine Essence is only known to the Divine Essence – there is no duality of subject and object, knower and known.

God is in everything, yet above all things, which is a description rather than a definition. But even such a definition (or a description) would contain, Ibn ʿArabī urges, definitions of all beings, actual and potential, physical and spiritual, and since a complete knowledge of everything is an impossibility for man, a complete definition of God is therefore impossible.

Ibn ʿArabī concludes by saying that the so-called attributes of transcendence (*ṣifāt al-tanzīh*) should be predicated of the Godhead (*al-ḥaqq*) not of the Essence, for the Essence, in its bare abstraction, is attributeless. The attributes of transcendence are summed up in what he calls absoluteness (*iṭlāq*), as contrasted with the limitedness (*taqyīd*) of the phenomenal world. To the Divine Essence explained above, Ibn ʿArabī sometimes applies the pronoun 'He', for the Essence alone is the absolute *ghayb* (unseen).

In short, Ibn ʿArabī says that we must distinguish two fundamentally different kinds of transcendence:

1. That which belongs to the Divine Essence *per se* and *a se* – the absolute simplicity and unity of the One – the state of the *aḥadiyya*.
2. Transcendence asserted by the intellect, which must always be coupled with immanence and which may assume the following forms:
   a. God may be called transcendent in the sense of being Absolute; or
   b. He may be called transcendent in the sense of being a necessary being, self-begotten, self-caused, etc., in contradistinction to the contingent, created or caused beings of the phenomenal world; or

c. He may be called transcendent in the sense that He is unknowable and incommunicable and beyond all proof.

The second kind of transcendence Ibn ʻArabī condemns if taken by itself (i.e. without immanence) to be an explanation of the whole truth about Reality. Reality as Ibn ʻArabī understands it has both aspects: transcendence and immanence.

CAUSALITY

"The movement of the creation of the world is an intelligible one", Ibn ʻArabī says. In consideration of this, 'cause' and 'effect' are mere appellations, two subjective categories.

As there is only one Reality, regarded in one aspect as a cause and in another as an effect, cause and effect are identical and every cause is an effect of its own effect; a conclusion which Ibn ʻArabī says would be pronounced impossible by the unaided intellect, but which, according to the mystic intuition, is an explanation of what actually is. The question is understood by the mystic as follows: every cause, on account of its being both an essence and a form, is both a cause and an effect, an agent and a patient; and every effect, on account of its being an essence and a form, is also both a cause and an effect, or an agent and a patient. And since Reality is One, now regarded as an essence, now as a form, it follows that It is both a cause and an effect at the same time, and that everything that is called a cause, on entering into a causal relation with anything else which is called an effect, is at the same time an effect of its own effect, on account of that effect being (by virtue of its essence) a cause. What it all amounts to is that God, who is the only cause, is immanent in both causes and effects, so it is immaterial whether we call a particular cause a cause of a certain effect, or an effect of this effect (itself being regarded as a cause).

According to Ibn ʿArabī, all changes in the phenomenal world, in fact all that he calls creation, is nothing but 'becoming'. He denies that the relation between God and the universe is a conditional relation on the ground that a condition (*sharṭ*) does not necessarily entail the existence of the thing of which it is a condition. For him, the existence of the universe is **necessarily entailed** by that of a necessary being. He argues that to be alive is a condition for being able to acquire knowledge and to have legs is a condition for being able to walk, but the existence of life does not necessarily entail that of knowledge, neither does the existence of legs necessarily entail walking. We can never say that the conditioned must exist, although we say that if it did, its condition must exist.

But unlike a condition, a cause, by itself, Ibn ʿArabī says, does entail the existence of its own effect. The universe is regarded by the Ashʿarites and the ancient philosophers as a necessary consequence of a certain cause. Ibn ʿArabī agrees with both, saying that we may say, following the Ashʿarites, that the divine knowledge of God, or the Essence, according to the philosophers, is the cause of the universe, if and only if this does not imply any **temporal** priority of God to the universe. It would be meaningless, he says, to talk about a temporal interval or a gap between the One and the Many, or God and the Universe, or the Necessary and the Contingent, if necessity and contingency are regarded (as he regards them) as only two aspects of the One. If we must say that the universe is caused or created at all, it must not be understood in the sense of the universe originated or created in time or from nothing. Ibn ʿArabī does not admit creation *ex nihilo*.

The world was never at any time a non-existent and then became an existent. The universe is eternal, infinite and everlasting, because it is the outward expression of the eternal, infinite and everlasting One. He says, "The end of the world is something unrealisable – neither has the world any ultimate goal". The so-called next world is something forever in the making. What people call this world and the next world are mere names for the ever new process of creation, which is a continual process of annihilation and recreation. There never is an interval in time. We cannot say that anything was not, then (*thumma*) was. 'Then' (*thumma*) does not mean an interval of time, but it indicates the logical priority of the cause to its effect. Ibn Rushd (Averroes), Ibn ʿArabī's contemporary and fellow countryman, explains creation as "renewed existence every instant in a constantly changing world, always taking its new form from the preceding". The universe as a whole is one big, contingent being. Neither the universe nor anything in it has an acquired existence in the sense of being created from nothing. Acquired existence is a mental fiction. What things acquire are the *aḥkām* (predications) of external existence.

Everything is an eternal existent in its state of latency (*thubūt*) and a temporal existent in its manifestation in the external world (*ẓuhūr*). He goes on to say that in saying that an object is created or caused to exist we mean no more than what we mean when we say that "a man has appeared in our house today", which does not imply that he had no previous existence before coming into our house. He says that God does not create anything; creation (*takwīn*) – which, according to him, means the coming into concrete manifestation of an already existing substance – belongs to the thing itself. "It comes to being" means that it manifests itself of its own accord. The only thing that God does in the matter is to **will** a thing to **be** (concretely manifested), and God wills nothing and commands nothing, the existence of which is not made necessary by the very nature and laws of things **themselves**. Were it not in the nature of a thing **to be** at the moment of God's command, it would never be. Nor even would God command it to be. So, nothing brings a thing into existence (i.e. makes its existence manifest) except itself.

He explains 'causality' in terms of two triads which correspond to one another, the one expressing one aspect of reality (God); the other, the other aspect (the phenomenal world). The first triad stands for God as a trinity of Essence, Will, and Word; the second stands for the phenomenal world, also a trinity, of essences characterised by obedience and hearing.

In this sense and this sense only does Ibn ʿArabī regard the universe as created or caused, just as it is in this sense that he calls it eternal. But there remains one fundamental point, which is that he denies the eternity of the world in one definite sense: that is in the sense that it is co-eternal with God in the form in which we know it. What is co-eternal with God, or what is God Himself, is the essence of the world, not the form. He says, "God predestines things in eternity but does not bring them into existence (i.e. in eternity), or what is the sense in calling Him a creator if the created things are co-eternal with Him?" In this sense, he calls the universe *ḥādith* (originated) and contingent and not-being, and he adds that it always is and always will be.

It is idle, he concludes, to ask when the world was created. 'When' refers to time, and time has always been regarded as a product of the phenomenal world itself. There is no temporal succession between creator and created, but there is a logical order of 'before' and 'after', not in time. Ibn ʿArabī adds that the relation between God and the universe is analogous to that of yesterday and today. "We cannot say that yesterday precedes today in time, since it is time itself. The non-existence of the world was never at any time."

The Divine Names

Ibn ʿArabī calls the Divine Names the causes of the universe. He regards the Divine Names as lines of force. As names of the Godhead, they demand by their very nature their logical correlatives, which can only be found in an outward expression or manifestation in the external world. The Knower, for example, demands something known; the Creator something created; and so on. Besides this, Ibn ʿArabī speaks of them as being instrumental causes (like tools) which God uses in all the creative activities in the world. Our knowledge of the Divine Names, he says, and of their hierarchical order – their classification into principal and subordinate – is the clue to our knowledge of the categories manifested in the spiritual and the physical worlds. In everything, no matter how complex it is, every 'aspect' (*wajh*) and every 'reality' (*ḥaqīqa*) corresponds and owes its very existence to a Divine Name, which is to this 'aspect' or 'reality' like a prototype. This is just repeating, in a different way, what he says about the phenomenal world being the attributes with which God is described. "God was, while the world was not, and He was named by all the Divine Names."

The Divine Essence is the One Universal Substance, identified with Absolute Reality. A Divine Name is the Divine Essence in one or other of its infinite aspects: a determinate 'form' of the Divine Essence. An Attribute is a Divine Name manifested in the external world; it is what Ibn ʿArabī calls a 'theatre of manifestation' for the Divine Substance to manifest itself in different degrees (*marātib*). In its absolute indeterminateness, the Divine Essence is a 'thing in itself'. It is indivisible, independent and unchanging. It is not a substance, but the One Substance which, in itself, embraces all substances, so-called material and non-material. What are fleeting, divisible and changeable are the 'accidents', the 'forms', the manifestations. The Attributes, according to him, have no meaning apart from the Divine Essence.

As forms and particularisations of the Divine Essence, the Divine Names are a multiplicity, each possessing unique characteristics by virtue of which it is distinguishable from the others, but essentially they are identical with the One Essence, and with one another.

Reality, which is ultimately one and indivisible in Ibn ʿArabī's doctrine, seems to be regarded from three different points of view in relation to our knowledge:

1. Reality as we know it, i.e. Reality as manifested in the external world. As such, it is subject to the limitations of our senses and intellects. We know it as a multiplicity of existents, and we assert of it relations of all kinds, causal or otherwise. This he calls the Phenomenal World, 'Appearance' and 'Not-Being', etc. But though an apparent multiplicity, the Phenomenal World is an essential unity, each part of which is the Whole and capable of manifesting all the realities of the Whole.
2. Reality such as we do not directly know or perceive, except by mystical intuition, but whose existence we logically infer (following our reason).

Of this, he maintains, we predicate attributes characteristic only of a Necessary Being, and Ibn ʿArabī chooses to call it God in a theistic sense – God as 'created in our beliefs'. This is only a fictitious and a subjective God and our conception of Him varies according to different individuals and communities, but according to Ibn ʿArabī any conception which deprives God of His absoluteness and universality, or renders His unity in any way incomplete by admitting the reality of any other deity or even of the Phenomenal World, is polytheistic. A complete conception of God, therefore, is one which comprises the two aspects of Reality (immanence and transcendence), i.e. of God as being both in and above the universe. This is the starting point in Ibn ʿArabī's Philosophy of Religion, as we shall see later.

We are forced to do this, he goes on to say, because the attributes we predicate of the Phenomenal World demand their logical correlatives: contingency demands necessity; relativity demands absoluteness; finitude demands infinity and so on. These logical correlatives can only be applied to a Reality thus conceived. "The key to the mystery of 'Lordship' is thou" (the phenomenal). The fundamental difference between Reality as conceived in (1) and in (2) is that in (1) the transcendental Attributes of God (*ṣifāt al-tanzīh*), which are the logical correlatives of the immanent Attributes (*ṣifāt al-tashbīh*), have no application. Attributes which express any relation between God and the Universe (in the orthodox sense) are explained away by Ibn ʿArabī, so we are really left with only two types of Attributes: transcendent, which are characteristic of God, and immanent, which are characteristic of the phenomenal world; each type explaining an aspect of Reality. We must not, therefore, predicate of God such attributes as 'green' or 'circular' or 'hearing' or 'seeing', etc., although His Essence is the essence of all that is green, circular and all that hears and sees.

What Ibn ʿArabī means by saying that, "we ourselves (including the phenomenal world) are the attributes with which we describe God", and, "there is not a single Name or Attribute with which He is characterised, the meaning or the spirit of which is not found in the phenomenal world" is, on the one hand, that the phenomenal world possesses unique characteristics which explain God's immanent side; and on the other, that through these characteristics we are formally led to ascribe to Him Attributes which explain His transcendent side. But regarding Reality as the Essence of All, all attributes whatever, transcendent and immanent, may be predicated of it. Ibn ʿArabī says, "He, may He be exalted, is (actually) named by all the names of the objects of the phenomenal world"; "Glory to Him who is 'meant' by all the attributes of the Godhead and created objects"; "Our names are His Names"; "He is called Abu Saʿid al-Kharrāz"; etc., etc.

3. Reality such as we do not directly know or perceive, but which, following our reason, we logically infer as we infer the existence of a substance when we perceive its accidents.

This is the Divine Essence, of which we can predicate nothing except bare existence. It is unknowable and incommunicable when regarded in abstraction and apart from any relation or limitation whatever. It is ultimately indefinable and, like a substance, it can only be described in terms of its 'states' which, in this case, are the phenomenal world. Its nature admits of no opposition or contradiction (*ḍidd*) or comparison (*mithl*), yet it unites in itself all opposites and similars. It has no qualities or quantities, yet it is the source of all qualities and quantities. It is generally referred to as 'Pure Light', or 'Pure Good', or 'the Blindness' (*al-ʿamā*).

This is the state of Uniqueness (*aḥadiyya*), which admits of no plurality whatever. As such, it is not an object of worship. The object of worship is the Lord (*al-Rabb*), not the Unique (*al-Aḥad*). But such unity becomes intelligible once we admit the other aspect, i.e. multiplicity, for, in itself, it transcends all multiplicity. It is the state of the 'One to Whom belong the burning splendours' (*al-subuḥāt al-muḥriqa*); that is, the One, the manifestation of Whom would cause all the multiplicity of phenomena to vanish, so that nothing would remain except the Real. He says, "The veil of the Unity (*al-aḥadiyya)* will never be removed; limit your hope, therefore, to the attainment (of knowledge) of the Oneness (*al-wāḥidiyya*), i.e. the unity of the Divine Names". No-one knows God as He really is (i.e. His Essence) except God, not even a mystic, for a mystic belongs to the multiplicity.

Ibn ʿArabī sometimes identifies the Divine Names with what he calls the *ḥaḍarāt* (Divine Presences), using the term *ḥaḍarāt* in a different sense from that in which it is used in connection with the five Divine *ḥaḍarāt* (Five Planes of Being). He enumerates only some of these, for according to him they are infinite in number. The 'Presence of the Godhead' (*al-haḍrat al-ilāhiyya*), for example, is the state in which God is revealed as *Allāh*; the 'Presence of the Merciful' is that in which He is revealed in the Name of the Merciful; and so on.

The only distinction Ibn ʿArabī makes between the One and the Many, or God and the Phenomenal World, which has already been explained, is expressed in a different way by what he calls the two aspects of the Divine Names. Regarded as a unity and as essentially one with the Divine Essence, the Names are said to be 'active' in the sense that each Name indicates one or other of the infinite lines of activity of the One. As a multiplicity manifested in the external world, i.e. regarded as the external world itself (for the external world is nothing other than the Divine Names) they are 'passive' and receptive. The former aspect he calls *taḥaqquq* (the point of view of the Real), the latter *takhalluq* (the point of view of the Created), and the relation between the two, through which actual manifestation is effected, is called *taʿalluq*. The Divine Names are also active when considered in relation to the *aʿyān al-thābita* (established potentialities), for these are nothing but the phenomenal world in latency; and in their turn, the *aʿyān al-thābita* are active in relation to the external world. It is all a hierarchy of higher and lower; the higher is active in relation to the lower and passive in relation to the one higher than itself.

There is but One Reality, which however much you multiply it (in thought) or try to conceive it, now as a multiplicity of existents, now as One Essence characterised by innumerable attributes and Names, remains in itself ultimately inconceivable and unalterable. All our knowledge of it is subjective and vain. There is no multiplicity, not even of Attributes or Names – no passivity or activity. These are terms which we ourselves have coined and found convenient to use for expressing what we choose to understand by Reality.

The *A'yān al-Thābita*

Ibn 'Arabī was the first to use the term *a'yān al-thābita* – which may be rendered 'fixed prototypes', or 'latent realities of things', or 'established potentialities' – in a more or less determined sense, and to give it a prominent place in a metaphysical system.

Before coming into concrete existence, things of the phenomenal world were in a state of potentiality in the Divine Essence of God and were – as ideas of His future 'becoming' – the content of His eternal knowledge, which is identical with His knowledge of Himself. God revealed Himself to Himself in a state of self-consciousness (not at any point of time) in what Ibn 'Arabī calls God's First Epiphany or Particularisation (*al-ta'ayyun al-awwal*), in which He saw in Himself and for Himself an infinity of these *a'yān* as determinate 'forms' of His own Essence – 'forms' which reflected and in every detail corresponded to His own eternal ideas of them.

These 'forms' are what Ibn 'Arabī calls the *a'yān al-thābita*. We may therefore define them as the latent states, both in the Mind and in the Essence of God, of His future 'becoming'; states which can only be expressed in terms of the Divine Names and all the possible relations which hold between them. The two-fold nature of these *a'yān*, i.e. their being intelligible ideas or concepts in the mind of God on the one hand, and particular 'modes' of the Divine Essence on the other, is explained by the fact that Ibn 'Arabī and his school use the terms *māhiyya* and *huwiyya* as equivalent to the term *'ayn al-thābita*. The one (*māhiyya*) explains the first aspect of the *'ayn*, i.e. its being an idea or a concept; the other (*huwiyya*), the second aspect, i.e. its being an essential 'mode'.

We can no more say that these *a'yān*, these potential 'modes' of the Essence, are other than the Essence or can have any existence apart from it, than say that mental states of our own minds are other than our minds, or can have any separate existence apart from them; or indeed, the states of any other substance whatever. Mentally, however, we may discriminate between the Essence and the *a'yān*, or the mind and its states, and think of them as apart. The *a'yān al-thābita* are in reality one with the Divine Essence and the Divine Consciousness. Yet, as 'states' or 'modes' they are no more the Divine Essence itself than our mental states are our minds.

Ibn 'Arabī calls them non-existent; not in the sense that they have no reality or being whatever, but in the sense that they have no external existence, or any existence apart from the Essence of which they are states. "Let it be known like this", Ibn 'Arabī says, "that the *a'yān al-thābita* are the images of the Divine Names and Qualities and 'things' of the Ipseity, in the Presence of Knowledge of the Ipseity, in whose image the Divine Essence is particularised and revealed in the Presence of Knowledge with specific individuation; they are established according to non-existence and they are not qualified by existence". **There is only one Reality – and a non-existent subjective multiplicity and non-existent subjective relations which limit and determine the One.**

The *a'yān al-thābita* are what Ibn 'Arabī calls the logical correlatives (*muqtaḍayāt*) of the Divine Names; but they are also potential essences. An interesting passage from Ibn 'Arabī's *Futūḥāt al-Makkīya* will explain his own view on the subject. "Is that", he asks, "which we call existent and perceive by our senses, the *'ayn al-thābita* 'transferred' from a state of non-existence to a state of existence? Or is it only its *ḥukm* (subjective determination) brought into an intelligible relation with the *'ayn* of the Real Being (God) – as a mirror image is related to a mirror – the so-called thing (external object) itself being a non-existent as it always was in its state of latency? (If the latter is the case), the *a'yān* of contingent beings must perceive each other only in and through the *'ayn* of the mirror of the Real Being; the *a'yān al-thābita* (these fixed prototypes) remaining as they always were in a state of non-existence."

"Or is it", he goes on to say, "that God manifests His being in (the forms of) these *a'yān*, which are to Him like theatres, so that each *'ayn* perceives the other when God manifests Himself in this other, a fact which is usually described as a thing having acquired existence *(istafāda'l-wujūd)* but which is nothing other than the manifestation or appearance of God in the form of that thing. This (second explanation) is nearer the truth in one respect; the other (explanation) is nearer the truth in another respect; but in both cases the *'ayn al-thābita* of the thing in question is a non-existent (externally) and still remains in its state of latency."

As potentialities and as intelligible ideas in the mind of God, they certainly are mere subjectivities; but as essences, they are all that is, since they are the Divine Essence Itself as particularised or determined. He says that God revealed Himself to Himself in 'the Most Holy Emanation' *(al-fayḍ al-aqdas)* in the forms of these *a'yān*. The 'Most Holy Emanation', with which we shall have to deal more fully later, is a continual process – in that it had no beginning and will never have an end – and potentialities in the One Essence are continually and unceasingly becoming actualities without any lapse in time, and they will continue to do so forever.

The Divine Consciousness embraces all the intelligible forms of the *a'yān*; the Essence, all their potential essences. Ibn 'Arabī often calls these essences spirits, and attributes to them functions and activities. God becomes conscious of Himself through the First Intellect, the *Rūḥ* (the Spirit), but He becomes conscious of each of the *a'yān* (each spirit) through the essences of the *a'yān* themselves, i.e. through the spirits which are particular 'modes' in the Universal Spirit.

Ibn 'Arabī's view about the identification of the knowledge of the One with the *a'yān* of things (the things themselves) is substantially the same as that of Plotinus. He identifies the Divine Knowledge with the Divine Essence, from which it follows that the Divine Knowledge is identical with all the potential 'modes' of the Essence, and that each 'mode' becomes identified with an idea of itself in the Divine Consciousness. In other words, each 'mode' must be at the same time a state in the Essence and a state in the Divine Knowledge, and the two states coincide and are in reality one in what Ibn ʿArabī calls the *ʿayn al-thābita.*

He calls the *aʿyān al-thābita* the 'keys of the Unseen' (*mafātīḥ al-ghayb*) and the 'first keys' (*mafātīḥ al-awwal*) because they were the opening chapter in the history of creation (although, strictly speaking, creation has no beginning or end); i.e. the revelation of the One to Himself as the Creator, contemplating in Himself the infinity of His creatures (His future manifestations). This particular state is known only to God Himself.

Ibn ʿArabī holds that it is not so impossible for a true mystic to obtain knowledge of the *aʿyān al-thābita* themselves, particularly his own *ʿayn*. He says, "Or it may be that God reveals to him (the mystic) his *ʿayn al-thābita* and its infinite succession of states, so that he knows himself in the same way that God knows him, having derived his knowledge from that same Source."

The *aʿyān al-thābita* have the unique characteristic of being both active and passive (or 'receptive'). Inasmuch as they are, in one sense, 'emanations' from the One and 'forms' of the Divine Names and potential 'modes' in the Divine Essence, they are passive and receptive (*qābil*). "The receptive (beings) come from nothing except His Most Holy Emanation", by which he means the *aʿyān al-thābita.* This Most Holy Emanation he also calls the Presence of Oneness, the Merciful Presence (*al-ḥaḍrat al-Raḥmāniyya*), the First Epiphany (*al-taʿayyun al-awwal*), the Presence of the Names (*ḥaḍrat al-asmāʾ*), the sphere of the spirits (*ʿālam al-arwāḥ*);

etc., etc. And in respect of their essences, that is by virtue of their possessing within themselves all the potentialities of becoming what the external existents of the phenomenal world are, they are regarded as active.

But activity and passivity here mean nothing more than logical determination (*ḥukm*). The *a'yān* are passive in relation to the Divine Names because of the *aḥkām* (determinations) which the Divine Names exercise over them; a state very analogous to the determination by a universal of its particulars. They are active in relation to the phenomenal objects in the same sense as a potentiality is active in relation to the actuality it becomes; i.e. in both cases it is only logical determination.

The Self-Revelations of the One

In his own few words, "Glory be to God Who created things, being Himself their essences". "He alone is proof of His own existence which is manifested in the *a'yān* of contingent beings." "There is nothing but God; nothing in existence other than He. There is not even a 'there' where the Essence of all things is one." "From whom dost thou flee and there is nought in existence but He?" "My eye sees nought but His Face (Essence), and my ear hears no other than His speech."

"Base the whole matter of your seclusion (*khalwa*) upon facing God with absolute unification, which is not marred by any (form of) polytheism, implicit or explicit; and by denying with absolute conviction all causes and intermediaries, whole or part; for verily if you are deprived of such *tawḥīd*, you will be bound to fall into polytheism." He denies becoming one with God. There is no 'becoming' whatever, but there is the realisation of the already existing fact that you are one with God.

"So on Him alone we depend for everything; our dependence on other things is in reality dependence on Him; for they are nothing but His appearances. Bayazid once asked God, "O Lord, with what can I draw nigh to Thee?", whereupon God replied, "With that which does not belong to Me", to wit, servility and dependence.

"For He, glory to Him", Ibn ʿArabī says, "has no resemblance whatever to His creation. His Essence cannot be apprehended by us, so we cannot compare it with tangible objects, neither are His actions like ours." "The movement of all existence is circular; it returns where it begins." He says that the 'movement' of the creation of the world originated through the essential love of the One to manifest Itself in external realities. "I was a hidden treasure, and I loved to be known so I created the world that I might be known".

The *tajalliyāt* (self-revelations or manifestations) are the different ways in which the One manifests Himself to us in the course of our knowledge of Him. *Tajallī* is "the eternal and everlasting self-manifestation"; the "overflowing of existence from the Essence to the forms; not in the sense of two vessels pouring, the one into the other, but in the sense of the One conceived now as an Essence, now as a form". That the universe is related to Him as an emanation is contrary to the nature of the Absolute. Absoluteness implies freedom from all relations.

There is One Reality which reveals or manifests Itself in an infinity of forms; not one that produces or creates, or one from which anything other than Itself emanates. Even the phrase 'manifestation in forms' is misleading, for the Essence and forms never stood apart, except in our thought. The First Intellect, Universal Soul, Universal Nature, etc., are not separate existents or in any way independent of one another, but different ways of viewing the One: i.e. the One regarded as Universal Consciousness; the One as Active Principle in the universe; the One as Life-giving Principle; the One as concretely manifested in the Phenomenal World; and so on.

The self-revelations of the One (*al-tajalliyāt*), thus understood, are as follows. When we conceive the One as apart from all possible relations and individualisations, we say that God has revealed Himself in the state of Unity (*al-aḥadiyya*) or is in the Blindness (*al-'amā*, non-communication) – the state of the Essence. When we regard it in relation to the potential existence of the phenomenal world, we say that God has revealed Himself in the state of the Godhead (*al-martaba al-ilāhiyya*). This is the state of the Divine Names. And when we regard it in relation to the actual manifestations of the phenomenal world, we say that God has revealed Himself in the state of Lordship (*al-rubūbiyya*).

If regarded as the Universal Consciousness containing all intelligible forms of actual and potential existents, we say that Reality revealed Itself in the First Intellect; and God revealed Himself as the Inward or the Unseen, and we call this state *ḥaqīqat al-ḥaqā'iq* (Reality of Realities). But if regarded as actually manifested in the phenomenal world, we say that God has manifested Himself in forms of the external world, and we identify Him with the Universal Body (*al-jism al-kulli*). When we think of Him as the Universal Substance which receives all forms, we say that God revealed Himself as Prime Matter (*al-hayūlā),* which Ibn 'Arabī sometimes calls *al-kitāb al-mastūr* (the Inscribed Book); and so on and so on.

The Reality of Realities

The Logos may be understood from many different points of view. As a purely metaphysical category it is called the First Intellect. From the mystical point of view it is called the Perfect Man, regarding it as the active principle in all divine and esoteric knowledge. In relation to Man, the Logos may be identified with the Real Man, while in relation to the universes it may be called the Reality of Realities. As a registry of everything it is called the Book (*al-kitāb*) and the Most Exalted Pen (*al-qalām al-ā'lā*). As the Essence whence everything takes its origin, it is called the *hayūlā* and the First Substance. The greatest danger is to forget that these terms refer to different aspects of the One Being, rather than to different beings.

The objects of all our knowledge, Ibn 'Arabī says, fall under three metaphysical categories:

1. Absolute Being which exists *per se* and is the origin of all that exists;
2. Contingent being which exists through the Absolute Being – otherwise it is 'not-being'; this is the universe;
3. Being which is neither existent nor non-existent, neither eternal nor temporal; it is co-eternal with the eternal and temporal with the temporal. Of this category of Being we can no more assert that it is prior to the universe than say God Himself is. It is prior to the universe, but its priority is only logical – without time priority. It is the inward aspect of the Godhead and the Godhead is its outward aspect. This is the 'Reality of Realities' or 'Idea of Ideas', the *Summum Genus*, the First Intellect and so on. It comprehends all ideas and all existing things absolutely. It is neither a whole nor a part, neither does it increase nor decrease. It is indefinable. It stands as near as possible to Matter. It multiplies with the multiplication of existents but does not divide (except in thought).

One could say it is God or the universe, but one could also say that it is neither. From it the universal proceeds as a particular proceeds from a universal. It contains the realities (ideas being identified with realities, *ḥaqā'iq*) of diverse objects; yet in itself it remains homogeneous. It stands in the closest relation to God's knowledge. It is known to God through itself, i.e. it is the consciousness of God. It is not the divine knowledge itself, but rather the content and substance of such knowledge. In it the knower, the known and the knowledge are one. Through it the universe is brought to manifestation. It is the 'store' of intelligible and archetypal ideas of the world of 'becoming'.

The Reality of Realities thus described is no more other than God than a potentiality, which under certain conditions becomes an actuality, can be called other than this actuality. It is God conceived as the Self-revealing Principle of the universe; God as manifesting Himself in a form of universal consciousness, at no particular time or place, but as the Reality which underlies all realities, and as a Being whose consciousness is identical with His Essence.

The Reality of Realities is completely manifested in the world which 'reflects' its positive being. It is perfect, and the universe which manifests its perfection is perfect. But while the universe manifests this perfection analytically, Man alone (the Perfect Man; not Animal Man) manifests it synthetically. Ibn ʿArabī attributes to this Reality of Realities (or First Intellect, etc) a creative activity which is very much analogous to the volitional activity of Man – but we have already seen what he means by creation and God as the Creator. It has, he says, the same relation to the latent realities of things (*al-aʿyān al-thābita*) as that which our minds have to their volitional states. Besides this creative activity, Ibn ʿArabī attributes to the Reality of Realities rationality. It is through it, as we have already seen, that God becomes conscious of Himself. Like Plotinus, Ibn ʿArabī believes that "to think itself belongs to the mind (which is *ḥaqīqat al-ḥaqā'iq*) not to the One". This consciousness has reached its highest point in the Perfect Man, in whom the object of creation is realised – the love of God to be known; and it is in the Perfect Man that God knows Himself perfectly.

The Reality of Realities marks the first step by which the Absolute is removed from its absoluteness in the process of its descent (to our knowledge). It is the First Epiphany of God, to whom God addressed Himself – as the Tradition of the Prophet says – "I have not created a creature dearer to Me than thee; with thee I give and with thee I take and with thee I punish".

The Perfect Man

No treatment of Ibn ʿArabī's doctrine of the Logos is complete which does not take into consideration his views of the Perfect Man, for this explains the practical aspect of his Logos: its relation to and manifestation in Man. His theory of the Logos therefore, presented in its completest form, comprises the following elements:

1. The Logos as the Reality of Realities: the metaphysical aspect;
2. The Logos as the Reality of Muḥammad: the mystical aspect;
3. The Logos as the Perfect Man: the human aspect.

The Principle of Universal Reason is immanent in everything and constitutes, as it were, the Divine Consciousness, hitherto identified with the Reality of Realities and the Reality of Muḥammad; but is not present in all beings in an equal degree. Man is the only being in whom this Principle is manifested in so high a degree that he deserves to be called the Viceregent of God (*al-khalīfa*) and the Image of God (*al-ṣūra*) and the Microcosm (*al-kawn al-jāmiʿ*); or the mirror which reflects all the perfections and Attributes of God; or even

God Himself. Ibn ʿArabī puts it all very boldly in the following passages:

a. Only two beings rightly call themselves God: God Himself who calls Himself *Allāh* in His Books; and the Perfect Man (*al-ʿabd al-kāmil*) like Bayazid; and

b. "When God, glory to Him, in respect of His Most Beautiful Names which are beyond enumeration, willed to see their *aʿyān*, or if you like you may say, His *ʿayn*, in a universal being (*kawn jāmiʿ*) which contains the whole matter (of creation) inasmuch as it is endowed with all aspects of existence, and through which the mystery of God is manifested to Himself, for the vision which consists of a thing seeing itself by means of itself is not the same as that of the thing seeing itself in something else which serves as a mirror for it..." Adam is the very 'polishing' of this mirror and the spirit of this form (in which God manifested Himself, i.e. Man) and the Angels are some of the 'powers' of that form, i.e. the universe, which the Sufis call the 'Great Man' (*al-insān al-kabīr*).

This is not the 'animal' man (*al-insān al-ḥayawānī*) but the 'rational' man – the Perfect Man in the strict sense in which Ibn ʿArabī uses the term – the class under which all Prophets and Saints are included, or the 'Gnostics' in the fullest sense of the word.

Everything manifests the Universal Rational Principle in a measure proportionate to its capacity. Even the so-called inanimate beings manifest this hidden rationality inasmuch as they obey their own inner laws. The whole creation is a rational structure from the lowest mineral to the highest type of man (the Perfect Man).

"No-one", Ibn ʿArabī says, "knows the dignity of Man and his place in the universe except those who know how to contemplate God perfectly." He is the only creature in whose power lies the possibility of knowing God absolutely. In fact it is through him that God knows Himself, for he is the manifested consciousness of God. Other beings know as much of the nature of God as they do of themselves, for the phenomenal objects are nothing but His Attributes. Their knowledge is imperfect and incomplete compared with that of Man, who sums up in himself **all** of God's Attributes.

Even the Angels' knowledge of God is imperfect. They know God as a transcendent Reality which has no relation to the phenomenal world. Man alone knows God both as the Real (*ḥaqq*) and the phenomenal (*khalq*), for Man himself (the Perfect Man) is the Real and the phenomenal, the internal and the external, the eternal and the temporal. The heart of the Perfect Man is the seat of the manifestation of the Universal Logos (the Reality of Realities or Reality of Muḥammad, etc.) and in it alone the activities of this Logos find their fullest expression. The Perfect Man is in immediate contact with Reality and through him the essential unity of the universal and the particular are realised.

Ibn ʿArabī, as well as Jīlī who follows him very closely on this subject, says that through the Perfect Man alone all God's perfections are revealed. "Perfect Man is", Ibn ʿArabī says, "the Divine unity (*al-jamʿiyya al-ilāhiyya*), i.e. all the Attributes pertaining to the Divine Presence (*al-janāb al-ilāhī*) and the Reality of Realities and the World of Nature."

A Perfect Man is not perfect, in his theory, unless he realises his essential oneness with God. This is what distinguishes any man from a Perfect Man. Every man is a microcosm in this sense, but only **potentially** so. The Perfect Man does actually manifest all God's Attributes and perfections, and such manifestation is incomplete without the full realisation of his essential unity with God. It follows, therefore, that every Perfect Man must be a mystic, in Ibn ʿArabī's sense, since in mysticism alone can such realisation be attained.

We have already seen that Ibn ʿArabī calls the Perfect Man the inward and the outward aspects of Reality. The essence of the Perfect Man is a mode of the Divine Essence. His spirit is a mode of the Universal Spirit. His body is a mode of the Universal Throne (*al-ʿarsh*). His knowledge is a reflection of the Divine Knowledge. The heart of the Perfect Man corresponds to the celestial archetype of *al-Kaʿba (al-bayt al-maʿmūr)*. His spiritual faculties correspond to the Angels; his memory to Saturn; his understanding to Jupiter; his intellect to the Sun; and so on and so on.

Like the Universal Logos which the Perfect Man manifests, the Perfect Man is called by Ibn ʿArabī an intermediary stage (*barzakh*); not in the sense of being an entity between God and the Universe, the Divine and the Human, but in the sense of being the only creature which unites and manifests both perfectly. Ibn ʿArabī explains the mystery of creation by saying that it was due to the essential love of the One to be known and to be manifested that God revealed Himself in the forms of the phenomenal world.

This eternal love of the One to behold His own Beauty and Perfections manifested in forms, and above all things to be known to Himself in and through Himself, found, Ibn ʿArabī says, its completest realisation in the Perfect Man, who alone knows Him and manifests His Attributes perfectly. He knows Him "in a manner which surpasses all doubt; nay, he perceives Him in the innermost 'eye' of his soul".

"He is to God what the eye-pupil is to the (physical) eye... and through him God beholds His creatures and has mercy upon them, i.e. creates them." It is in this sense that Ibn ʿArabī calls the Perfect Man the cause of creation, for in the Perfect Man alone the object of creation is realised. Were it not for Man (the Perfect Man) creation would have been purposeless, for God would not have been known; so it was for the sake of the Perfect Man that the whole creation was made, i.e. that God manifested Himself both in the world and in the Perfect Man.

The dignity of Man, therefore, cannot be overrated in Ibn ʿArabī's view. Man is the highest and most venerable creature

God ever created. He should be guarded and honoured, for **"he who takes care of Man takes care of God"**. Ibn 'Arabī also says, "The preservation of the human species should have a much greater claim to observance than religious bigotry, with its consequent destruction of human souls, even when it is for the sake of God and the maintenance of the law." **"God has so exalted Man"**, Ibn 'Arabī adds, **"that He placed under his control all that is in the heavens and the earth, from its highest to its lowest."**

Not only does Ibn 'Arabī regard Man (the Perfect Man) as the cause of the creation of the universe in the sense just explained, but also as the preserver and maintainer of the universe. "The universe continues to be preserved so long as the Perfect Man is in it." "Dost thou not see that when he departs and is removed from the treasury of the present world, there shall not remain in it (in the world) that which God has stored therein, and that which was in it shall go forth and each part shall become one with each other and the whole affair shall be transferred to the next world and shall be sealed everlastingly?"

It seems that when Ibn 'Arabī calls the Perfect Man the preserver and the controller of the whole universe in a real sense, he means either the Perfect Man as identifying himself with the *Nous* in the mystic experience of *fanā'*, i.e. the Divine Man; or the *Nous* (the Reality of Realities) itself, i.e. God as the Creative and Rational Principle.

Ibn 'Arabī was the first to put forth a synthetic and systematic theory, or rather a group of theories, derived from different sources and brought into one unity. Not only was he the first to expound such a doctrine, he was also the last to produce a Logos-doctrine of any importance. All those who came after him simply reproduced his ideas in some form or another, sometimes even *verbatim et litteratim*.

The emphasis laid on the trinity as the fundamental Principle in all the productive or creative activities of the Universal

Logos bears a Christian stamp. But it was not Christianity itself which influenced Ibn ʿArabī, rather that all manifestation requires three relationships. Ibn ʿArabī's trinity was only a trinity of relative aspects, not of three Persons. Even the reality of Muḥammad is threefold; syllogistic reasoning must have three elements; and he expresses this idea very daringly in the following line, "My Beloved is three, although He is One".

There is a striking resemblance between the philosophy of the Logos as described by Philo of Alexandria and that of Ibn ʿArabī. Ibn ʿArabī uses the term Logos (*kalima*), to mean both eternal wisdom (as the term originally meant in Greek philosophy) and the 'Word' (or 'speech' as the term means in Hebrew).

Philo's terminology	**Ibn ʿArabī's terminology**
The High Priest	*imām* or *qutb*
The Intercessor	*al-shāfiʿ*
The Glory of God	The Man who is the Reality (*insānu ʿayn al-ḥaqq*)
The Shadow of God	The Image of Truth (*habā* or *sūrat al-ḥaqq*)
Idea of Ideas	Reality of Realities (*ḥaqīqat al-ḥaqāʾiq*)
The Intermediary	The Isthmus (*barzakh*)
Principle of Revelation	Reality of Muḥammad
First Born Son of God	First Epiphany (*taʿayyun al-awwal*)
The First of the Angels	The Spirit (*rūḥ*)
Viceregent	*khalīfa*
Divine Man	Perfect Man

Sainthood

Wilāya (sainthood), according to Ibn ʿArabī, and indeed according to a great majority of Sufis, does not mean holiness or piety, although such characteristics may be found in a saint. The distinguishing mark of *wilāya*, as Ibn ʿArabī understands it, is 'gnosis' (*maʿrifa*). In other words, a man is a saint if he is what Ibn ʿArabī calls a Perfect Man. Ibn ʿArabī extends the meaning of the term saint (*walī*) so as to include the following:

1. All prophets and apostles
2. Some Sufis
3. The 'Singular Men' (*al- afrād*) like ʿAbd al-Qādir al-Gīlānī
4. The Guards (*al-umanāʾ*)
5. The Beloved (*al-aḥbāb*)
6. The Heirs (*al-waratha*) etc.

He also uses the term *walī* (saint) to include all apostles and prophets. An apostle, according to him, is pre-eminently a saint who is charged with the external duty of delivering a message from God, and a prophet is a saint who is distinguished from the rest of the sainthood on account of his possessing unique knowledge of the Unseen Worlds.

Wilāya (sainthood), thus explained, is the basis of all spiritual ranks and the only element common to all of them. It is, Ibn ʿArabī adds, originally a Divine Attribute, for God calls Himself *al-Walī*, and if we apply the term to men it is only to those who have realised their essential oneness with Him. It is more general than either Prophecy (*nubuwwa*) or Apostleship (*risāla*): Prophecy and Apostleship are particular grades of it. It is a permanent state, while Prophecy and Apostleship are only temporary. The knowledge which belongs to it is infinite, for it is identical with God's Knowledge and with that of the Spirit of Muḥammad; whereas prophetic and apostolic knowledge is finite.

The Universal Logos, as identifying itself in Ibn ʿArabī's Logos-doctrine with the Spirit or Reality of Muḥammad, explains what is meant by the General Viceregency. The real Viceregent (*khalīfa*) of God is the Muḥammedian Spirit, which is forever manifesting itself in the form of prophets and saints (the class of people coming under the category of the Perfect Man), each of whom may be called a *khalīfa*. They all manifest this General Viceregency. We may call them all saints, for according to Ibn ʿArabī, every prophet and every apostle is, in one of his aspects, a saint. All these saints (using the term in the widest sense), Ibn ʿArabī says, 'derive' such knowledge as constitutes their sainthood (i.e. esoteric knowledge) from the Spirit of Muḥammad. In addition to this, *wilāya* is more perfect. Ibn ʿArabī does not mean that any saint whatever is more perfect than, or superior to, any prophet or apostle, but rather that the saintly side of a prophet or an apostle is superior to his prophetic or apostolic side.

In this way all apostles, prophets and saints belong to one and the same group, with one common element uniting them all – this element being the active principle in all revelation and inspiration: the Logos, the Muḥammedian Spirit. He even goes so far as to say that all religions (*sharāʾiʿ*) of the prophets from Adam to Muḥammad are nothing but temporal manifestations, according to the requirements and needs of the human race at different times, of the one universal religion which he calls Islam (using the term to mean all religions, including Islam itself).

Knowledge

Not only does knowledge vary in kind, but the channels through which knowledge is obtained are different. Ibn 'Arabī gives a classification of propositions (or judgements expressed in propositions) based on this principle. He holds that normally all knowledge is obtained through six faculties: the five senses and the intellect, counting the intellect as a faculty. They are, he says, numerically different, but essentially one. But there are, he adds, people who do not obey this normal law of things: they acquire all kinds of knowledge through only one or other of the senses, and some acquire it through no sense or faculty whatever. He regards as abnormal the knowledge resulting from clairvoyance, telepathy, hypnotism, and, above all, the kind of knowledge he calls intuitive or esoteric.

Broadly speaking Ibn 'Arabī divides all propositions or judgements into two main classes:

1. Necessary judgements, under which he includes:
   - (i) All perceptual judgements (purely perceptual, i.e. without the interference of the understanding);
   - (ii) Some intellectual judgements, by which he seems to mean the a priori self-evident propositions of pure mathematics and formal logic;
   - (iii) All intuitive judgements (esoteric judgements).
2. Contingent judgements, under which he includes judgements based on the understanding and the senses together.

By necessary judgements Ibn 'Arabī means judgements which are necessarily true. Contingent judgements may be true, but their truth is not necessary. Perceptual judgements, he would say, may be regarded as false on the ground that they do not correspond to objective realities, but he still calls them necessarily true in the sense that they correspond to something. When a man asserts that he is seeing a pink rat, his judgement is true, in Ibn ʿArabī's view, in the sense that the man must have seen something; i.e. the man's perception must have been conditioned by something objective. To call this 'something' a pink rat is not the fault of the senses, but of the understanding. All illusions, like the phenomenon of the mirage, would be explained by Ibn ʿArabī in this way. Judgements which do not correspond to external realities, and are not conditioned by any external objects whatever, are fabrications of imagination, and are therefore necessarily false.

Now if we imagine, Ibn ʿArabī goes on to say, a mental power which would govern the intellect in the same way as the understanding governs the senses, it would be conceivable that such a power might err with regard to the intellect, in the same way as the understanding errs with regard to the senses; i.e. that such a power would be likely to pronounce some of the self-evident propositions of the intellect to be false, when they appear to the intellect to be necessarily true. Ibn ʿArabī does not tell us whether there is such a power, but what he wishes to emphasise is the fact that necessary knowledge of the kinds mentioned above is true in itself, and that it is due to the erring judgement of the understanding, or some other 'judge' (*ḥakam*), that it is sometimes pronounced false.

Of the three kinds of necessary knowledge the third, intuitive knowledge, is the most important. It forms the kernel of Ibn ʿArabī's mystical philosophy of knowledge. Like the rest of the mystics, he believes in the possibility of a kind of knowledge most unlike that of discursive reason. It is the immediate perception, not of an external object this time, but of the Truth Itself; i.e. knowledge of the realities of things as they are, as contrasted with the probable and merely conjectural knowledge of the intellect.

Ḥallāj asserted long before Ibn ʿArabī that the human intellect is incapable of comprehending realities. "Thoughts are mere ideas of relations." True knowledge proceeds directly from the Universal Soul to the particular souls, or as Ḥallāj puts it, "from the Light to the light." Ḥallāj draws a distinction between knowledge of the Real and knowledge of the phenomenal, which correspond to what he calls Length (*ṭūl*) and Breadth (*ard*). To know the Real is to see for yourself; knowledge of the understanding is limited and indirect. It is very much similar to Spinoza's third kind of knowledge (*Scientia intuitiva*) which, as Spinoza says, is a state in which the human consciousness is absorbed in the *Amor intellectualis Dei*.

The Sufis themselves were wise in calling this kind of knowledge 'taste' (*dhawq*), an act of cognition. Sometimes they call it the Divine Knowledge (*ʿilm ladunnī*) and knowledge of the Mysteries (*ʿilm al-asrār*) and knowledge of the Unseen (*ʿilm al-ghayb*) and "knowledge of the people who, in this world, possess the nature of the next world", like prophets and saints, etc. The unseen (*al-ghayb*) is of two kinds: the Absolute *ghayb*, i.e. the Divine Essence which is unknowable; and the relative *ghayb*, knowledge of which is possible for some and impossible for others.

Ibn ʿArabī divides knowledge into three kinds: knowledge of the intellect (*ʿilm al-ʿaql*), knowledge of the states (*ʿilm al-aḥwāl*) and knowledge of the Mysteries (*ʿilm al-asrār*). Under divine knowledge, or knowledge of mysteries, he includes such things as instinctive knowledge and knowledge of inanimate beings, since he believes that even inanimate beings know God and glorify Him.

We may therefore use the terms intuition, or insight, or immediate perception of the truth, or indeed any other term for divine knowledge, provided we distinguish it from other kinds, particularly reflective thinking.

The following seem to be the most outstanding characteristics of esoteric knowledge as understood by Ibn ʿArabī:

1. Esoteric knowledge is innate; that of the intellect is acquired. It belongs to the Divine Effulgence (*al-fayḍ al-ilāhī)* which illuminates the very being of all creatures. It manifests itself in man under certain mystical conditions, e.g. perfect passivity of mind. The mystic is advised to be so passive in his thinking that he reaches the state of inanimate things. It is not the outcome of any practice or discipline: it lies dormant in the deepest recesses of the human heart.
2. It is beyond reason, and we should not invoke the authority of reason to test its validity. On the contrary, if reason and intuition should conflict, the former should always be sacrificed to the latter. If what prophets and saints tell us seems incompatible with our reason, we should take the word of the prophet and the saint for granted; reason is no judge of such truth. Reason may be right sometimes, but Ibn ʿArabī holds that its rightness is accidental. Reason should not interfere with divine knowledge or attempt to interpret it.
3. It manifests itself in the form of light which floods every part of the heart of the Sufi when he attains a certain degree of spiritual purification. Discipline is necessary only insofar as it helps to remove the 'veils' which pertain to the animal soul, and which prevent the heart from reflecting its eternal knowledge and perfections.
4. Esoteric knowledge materialises itself only in certain men. **"There is none amongst us but has his appointed place."** So all that is meant by *kashf* (revelation), according to Ibn ʿArabī, is simply the unveiling. When the veils are lifted up, the 'eye of the heart' sees all things – eternal and temporal, actual and potential – as they really are in their state of latency (*thubūt*).

5. Unlike speculative knowledge, which at most yields probability, intuition yields certain knowledge. The former has for its object the shadow of the Real, the phenomenal world; the latter, Reality itself. The only way of obtaining such knowledge is by means of 'immediate vision' (*shuhūd*) of realities. God's knowledge is *shuhūd* and so is the knowledge of those whom He favours.

6. It is essentially identical with God's knowledge, and though it appears to be of various kinds, it is essentially one. That it is essentially God's knowledge is proved by the fact that no-one attains it unless he has already attained the mystic station wherein esoteric knowledge is revealed and wherein he realises his essential oneness with God, i.e. the state of *fanā'*, in which God becomes (without any prior severance) the hearing, sight and all the other faculties of the mystic. This is God's knowledge, obtained in and through God. It is also our knowledge of Him, through Him. This point will be treated more fully in connection with Ibn 'Arabī's theory of *fanā'*. As for its being essentially one kind, Ibn 'Arabī holds that although it appears to come through different channels, it springs from one common source. The knowing substance which is the essence (*huwiyya*) of all human faculties is one and its knowledge is therefore one. Pure Light (which is also Pure Being) is the source of all knowledge. The senses and all other human faculties are media through which this Light manifests itself. Light is the only apprehending (*mudrik*) Principle in all conscious beings; the only thing that is visible in itself and makes other things visible.

7. Esoteric knowledge is ineffable. It is like sense perceptions and feelings, i.e. it cannot be known except by immediate experience. You can no more explain the knowledge revealed by a mystical experience to a person who has not gone through the experience, than you can explain what 'red' means to a blind man. No-one but a mystic can realise the full meaning of such knowledge, and the only way

to describe it is to explain it, as mystics have always done, by means of ambiguous and misleading metaphors. "The vision is there", Plotinus says, "for him who will see it."

8. Through it the mystic gains perfect knowledge of Reality. The unaided intellect asserts absolute transcendence of God. The mystic asserts both transcendence and immanence. He sees through the Divine *tajallī* how the One permeates the Many, and knows in what sense the One is different from the Many. This, Ibn 'Arabī believes, is the doctrine preached in all divine religions and sanctioned by *awhām* (conjecture). The transcendence which the mystic asserts of God is not the same as that of the philosophers. It is the absoluteness of the One which is revealed to the mystic in his vision. It is not based on inference or logical deduction. "It is", as Jāmī says, "like knowing Zayd personally – the other is like knowing him by name."

The philosopher can never hope to know more about causality than what he observes or infers from observation of causal happenings in the external world. The believer, on the other hand, sees for himself how the One Cause operates in all. Again, the philosopher cannot go beyond asserting the absolute transcendence of God; the believer knows by taste (*dhawq*) both aspects of Reality, i.e. transcendence and immanence. In one of his mystical states, the believer (who is also a mystic) realises his essential oneness with the Real, a state in which the knower and the known become one; this is beyond the reach of the philosopher altogether.

The Heart

Like the rest of the Sufis, Ibn ʿArabī metaphorically calls the human 'heart' the instrument through which esoteric knowledge is transmitted, or the centre wherein it is revealed. It is not the heart itself (i.e. not the hollow and the conic piece of flesh situated in the chest) that is meant by this instrument; it is something else which, "though connected with it physically and spiritually, is different from it and other than it". The word 'heart' is only a symbol for the rational aspect of Man – the Spirit. It is not identical with the intellect (as understood by the philosophers), which Ibn ʿArabī definitely regards as phenomenal and dependent on the body; but rather it is an inseparable 'part' of the Principle of Universal Reason which, though it functions through a body, is neither the body itself, nor dependent on a body for its existence, nor bound in any way by material limitations.

This mysterious power has, he says, a more mysterious faculty that he calls the 'inward eye' (*ʿayn al-baṣīra)* which, like the physical eye, perceives things, but the object of its perception is Reality itself. The things that blind this inward eye are the evil thoughts harboured by the animal soul, and all that pertains to the material world. Once freed from such veils, the heart of the mystic begins to comprehend the Real and communicate directly with the Rational Principle of the Universe.

The heart of the mystic is the same as the 'particular intelligence' of the philosophers, a term which Ibn ʿArabī sometimes uses to mean the rational soul and not the intellect. A particular intelligence, in his view, is a mode – or as he puts it a 'particularisation' – of the Universal Reason. It is essentially identical with the Universal Soul but conceptually different from it. The relation between the two is the same as that between a universal and its particulars, or a continuant and its occurrents – rather the latter than the former. What multiplies the one soul is the same as that which multiplies the One Essence, i.e. subjective relations (*nisab*); otherwise, souls are not divisible. The particular souls are no more parts of the Universal Soul than mental states are parts of a mind. Ibn 'Arabī uses a similar analogy when he calls particular intelligences 'powers of the Universal Soul'.

The term 'union' must always be taken in a metaphorical sense. How can there be a real union in a mystical experience when all particular souls are already united with the Universal Soul, which is God Himself? (God – the Rational Principle of the Cosmos). The so-called 'union', therefore, is but a state of 'waking up' for the particular soul and the realisation of the already existing union between itself and All-Soul, rather than an amalgamation of two different souls. According to Ibn 'Arabī the final achievement of the mystic, and the ultimate goal of his endeavours, is **not to become** one with God, for he already is, but to **realise** the meaning of such oneness. It follows that:

1. There is no real becoming at all: man never becomes God nor God man. The *"Anā'l-Ḥaqq"* (I am the Truth) of Ḥallāj is literally true in Ibn 'Arabī's view.
2. The so-called esoteric knowledge of the Sufis springs directly from the individual soul itself. It is not revealed or inspired in any real sense. All such terms as transmission and communication of knowledge must be understood metaphorically. The symbolic language used in this subject is here, as it is everywhere else, a great source of danger. If taken literally, it would suggest a duality of a revealer and a revealed to, a giver and a receiver of knowledge, and so on, whereas there is only the One. Ibn 'Arabī describes the First Intellect (a term which he uses as equivalent to the Universal Soul) in such a way, and attributes to it such characteristics, that it appears fundamentally different from particular intelligences. But we know that according to him the Universal Soul differs from particular souls only in the sense in which a whole differs from its 'parts'. He also speaks of the Spirit (*al-Rūḥ*), meaning

Gabriel, as identical with Universal Soul, as the only revealer of esoteric knowledge (*al-mulqī*), and brings numerous passages from the Qu'rān to bear on this point. What he really means, as he himself admits, is that it is the *Rūḥ* in its particular 'modes' that is the sole revealer; that revelation is the announcement of the soul (the particular soul) itself.

The mystic is said to receive knowledge in all the *ḥaḍarāt* (presences), but the giver of such knowledge is the self, which appears in different 'forms' according to the nature of each *ḥaḍra*.

Like Plotinus, whom he follows closely, Ibn ʿArabī believes in the essential unity of rational souls with the Universal Soul. The heart of the Sufi, or the rational soul thus conceived, is the eye, so to speak, whereby God sees Himself, and the instrument whereby He knows Himself in the forms of His manifestations. Man (the Perfect Man) is the focus of the divine consciousness of God; God is the focus and the essence of the consciousness of Man.

Reality, which is forever manifesting itself in an infinity of forms and in all planes of existence, is reflected, as if in a mirror, in the heart of the true Gnostic, who follows Reality everywhere and recognises it in everything. Every state of, or change in, the one eternal substance, corresponds to a state of, or a change in, the heart of the Gnostic. This is what Ibn ʿArabī means by saying that God is "contained in the heart of the Gnostic". It contains Him in two ways:

1. It reflects all the divine perfections which are separately manifested in the Macrocosm but collectively manifested in the Microcosm (Man).
2. It also contains God in the sense that it contains the divine (the essential or spiritual) aspect of Man, the only aspect by virtue of which Man may be called God.

But Ibn ʿArabī lays more stress on the former of these two senses, saying that this is the true meaning of the Prophetic Tradition, **"whoso knows himself knows his Lord".**

The Soul

Ibn ʿArabī recognises three distinct elements in Man, which he calls body, soul and spirit. He defines body as a material form which has extension in space and duration in time, and which is perishable and changeable. It is a particular 'mode' of the Universal Body *(al-jism al-kulli)*. Soul, on the other hand, is defined by him as the vital principle – the animal-life in the human organism. It is a particular 'mode' of Universal Soul (*al-nafs al-kulliya*). And lastly, he defines spirit as the rational principle, the purpose of which is to seek true knowledge. It is a 'mode' of Universal Intellect (*al-ʿaql al-kulli)*.

Ibn ʿArabī speaks of three distinct aspects of the soul: the vegetative, the animal and the rational. He definitely asserts that the vegetative and the animal souls are the body itself. They function through it, and depend for their very existence upon it. The rational soul, he says, is identical with neither the intellect nor the body, although **intellect is one of its subordinate 'powers'** and, during its association with body, it functions through it. It is independent of the body; it can actually exist apart from it, as it did before 'joining' it, and as it will do after parting with it.

"I do not mean by the spirit", he says, "the food-seeking instinct which resides in the liver; or that human power which responds to anger and passion; or the life-generating power lodged in the heart, a power usually called the animal soul, which manifests itself in sensations and movements and passions, etc; but I mean that perfect and simple substance which is living and active, whose sole activities are remembering, retaining ideas, comprehending, discriminating and reflecting." (Yet he does not identify it with the intellect.) "It is capable of receiving all kinds of knowledge and never becomes weary of receiving abstract ideas. This substance is the 'chief' of all the three souls and the prince (*amīr*) of all the powers which serve it and obey its commands." But he goes on to say, "It is neither a body nor an accident (*'arad*), but a substance belonging to the 'world of command' (*al-'ālam al-amr*, the spiritual world); and the Divine command is neither a body nor an accident, but a power like the First Intellect and the Universal Soul and other Pure Spirits. It is the reality signified by the word 'I'."

Death is no destruction, but a dissolution of 'parts' of the so-called material form. All 'frames' (or forms) are regarded by him as mere nothing – passing shadows – with a reality behind them which constitutes their very being. The human body is no exception to the rule. All the so-called three souls and the body are ultimately one. But the occult is more perfect and more venerable than the manifest; the rational soul in this case, being the hidden aspect of Man, occupies this honourable position. It is the 'part' of Man to which God addresses Himself, and the one that is expected to fulfil moral obligations.

Essentially, Ibn 'Arabī believes, the apprehending reality is one. This he calls the Light (*al-nūr*) without which nothing can apprehend or be apprehended. In Man this Light takes the form of the rational soul which we have already explained. Ibn 'Arabī insists on the unity of this principle (Light) not only in its cosmic functions as the operating 'Mind' in all spheres of intellection, but even in every individual being wherein it abides. Man hears, feels, tastes; he thinks, memorises, imagines; and above all receives knowledge of the unseen world, etc., by means of senses and faculties which people call by different names, but which, according to Ibn 'Arabī, are essentially one, i.e. this Light. "If you apprehend sound you call the apprehending Light 'hearing'; and if you perceive by sight, you call it 'seeing'; and so on to the end of the senses and faculties."

In short, Light, according to Ibn ʿArabī, is everything through which apprehension takes place. Not only that, but everything that is apprehended must have a special relation to the apprehending Light which is God. To put it in other words, God is all that apprehends and all that is apprehended. If a thing cannot be apprehended by a mind of some sort (not necessarily by a human mind) it cannot be reality at all. On this remarkable theory Ibn ʿArabī bases, with no inconsistency, both his empirical and his mystical psychology, normal and abnormal. The very Light which apprehends colours and sounds and conceives ideas and forms and images, etc., is the same as that which directly and immediately perceives Reality itself.

Ibn ʿArabī maintains that, though there is a difference between the intellect (*al-ʿaql*) and the rational soul (*al-rūḥ*), and between reflective thinking and immediate intuition, the difference cannot possibly be regarded as ultimate. If there is a difference at all, it is in the different ways in which this Light manifests itself. While the apprehending Light is perfectly free in mystical intuition, it is comparatively limited in reflective thinking and more tied down still by the limitations of the senses in sense perception.

The senses perceive through the agency of the apprehending Light, which forms their very essence and the essence of the objects perceived. Perceptual situations can be apprehended by the heart even in the absence of perceptible objects. It 'sees' them in itself as copies of the eternal Ideas of the Soul.

Concepts are innate ideas in the soul. "The soul is essentially a knowing substance"; soul is already born with these innate ideas. He speaks of the soul's forgetting its eternal knowledge during its temporary association with the body.

The so-called acquired knowledge is knowledge remembered by the soul. Some souls, like those of prophets and saints, never forget their knowledge and never experience that sickness (*maraḍ*) which befalls other souls.

Universal ideas are a common property of every human soul: Ibn ʿArabī maintains that they are innate in the human soul. He reduces all conceptual knowledge – all knowledge of the external world – to a simple relation between the already knowing soul (or its concepts) and the objects of the external world on the one hand; and to a process of relating these concepts themselves on the other. For example, to formulate the proposition 'a body is standing' is to relate in mind the notion of 'body' with that of 'standing', both of which are unchangeable ideas. The relation between them, taken in its universality, is also an unchangeable concept. Even the particular relation, i.e. that this body is standing now, is unchangeable in the sense that it (itself) cannot be asserted of any other body to which it does not belong. If we say that the particular relation does change, since the standing body might move the next moment, Ibn ʿArabī would answer that the body has entered into another relation altogether, and the previous relation has not changed. There are, therefore, four elements in all conceptual thinking:

1. Abstract relation (*nisba muṭlaqa*),
2. The object to which a relation is made (*al-mansūb ilayhi*),
3. The attribute related (*al-nisba*),
4. The particular relation (*al-nisba al-shakhṣiyya*).

The great hindrance to clear conceptual thinking, Ibn ʿArabī says, is the understanding, because it is always accompanied by images which tend to limit the universality of the universal concepts we have just explained.

Ibn ʿArabī draws a distinction between 'desire' (*shahwa*) and 'will' (*irāda*) by defining the former as the mere striving toward the gratification of some natural appetite or other. This striving is usually determined by the nature of its object. Will, on the other hand, for him, means a divine and spiritual power whose object is never an existing one (i.e. a concrete object in the external world). Will has an important bearing on what the Sufis call the mystic yearning or longing for their Beloved (God). Ibn Farīḍ and Ibn 'Arabī have talked about Absolute Beauty and Absolute Perfection as being the object (not in a concrete sense) of their love and contemplation, but no-one except a mystic can fully understand what love in abstraction or contemplation of the Absolute means.

Khayāl

Khayāl is used to mean any intermediary between two stages. He calls the Blindness (*al-'amā) khayāl* (illusory) because it is an intermediate stage between the Absolute Essence and the Phenomenal World. Mental images are *khayāl* because they are an intermediate stage between the spiritual and the visible world. Dreams are *khayāl* because they are a stage between the Real and the phenomenal life. Mirror images are *khayāl* because they are a species of their own: they are neither concrete objects nor abstract ideas.

We must be on our guard in understanding what Ibn 'Arabī says about *khayāl*, and we must also distinguish between at least two different kinds of it:

1. The psychological kind, i.e. mental images which are only seen in, and have no existence apart from, a mind. Under this category we may class dreams, illusions and ordinary normal images of waking life.
2. What we may call the metaphysical kind.

The first is divided by Ibn 'Arabī into two kinds:

a. Separable (*munfaṣil*) which is seen in the plane of imagination (*al-ḥaḍrat al-khayāl*) as having an external corporeality; like the forms of Gabriel seen by Muḥammad, and the serpent which was seen in place of Moses' staff.

For Ibn ʿArabī this is a different type of imagination from optical illusions (understood in a strictly psychological sense);

b. Inseparable (*muttaṣil*) by which he seems to mean ordinary mental images. This he divides into two more sub-classes:
   1. images which are consciously recalled to the mind by the process of *takhayyul*, and
   2. images which come to the mind of their own accord under certain conditions, e.g. in dreams.

Ibn ʿArabī's theory of *khayāl* is not purely psychological. *Khayālāt* are not only mind-dependent products which have no being in themselves, as a psychologist would say. There is a definite place allotted to them in Ibn ʿArabī's (and even in Ghazālī's) theory of being. Some *khayālāt*, e.g. the separable ones, belong, he says, to the 'Essential Presence' (*al-ḥaḍrat al-dhātiyya*) and are always ready to receive meanings (*maʿāni*) and spirits (*arwāḥ*). They are forms in which Reality reveals Itself to the human mind, and he even regards them as higher forms than those of the sensible world.

It would be desirable to recall what has been said about the inward 'eye of the heart' (*al-ʿayn al-basīra*), for it is, according to Ibn ʿArabī, the only key to the spiritual world in Man's possession. Revelations and inspirations, which we have hitherto explained as springing directly from the heart, are sometimes, he says, given to the mystic or the prophet in the form of a dream. This is a veridical dream (*al-ruʾyā al-ṣādiqa*), but there are other dreams which belong to a different class altogether.

Ibn ʿArabī holds that the faculty of imagination is always active, whether in waking life or in sleep. During waking hours this faculty is too distracted by sense impressions to do its work properly, but in sleep, when the senses and other faculties are in a state of rest, the imagination fully awakes. Sometimes it acts on images connected with ordinary events of the everyday life of the individual and presents them to the 'inward eye' of the heart, which reflects them and magnifies them like a mirror. In this way ordinary dreams are caused. They are just associations of ideas and images connecting themselves with some objects of desire.

But sometimes the 'Guarded Table' (by which Ibn ʿArabī means the Universal Soul) reveals itself, with all it contains of archetypal ideas, to the rational soul of man. What he means here is that the rational soul of man, which is a mode of the Universal Soul, is revealing itself to itself. The imagination seizes such ideas and acts upon them even in such a state. The heart (now in immediate contact with the Universal Soul) becomes, Ibn ʿArabī says, like "a running yet undefiled stream, wherein are reflected illuminated objects of all descriptions". The person to whom such a dream is revealed only sees the reflections in this stream, which are symbols of realities that lie behind them.

Ibn ʿArabī holds that although such dreams are veridical, they must be interpreted because they are symbolic. It is the imagination that supplies the symbols, and we must not take symbols for realities. When the Prophet saw milk in a dream, he only saw a symbol. The reality behind it was knowledge.

Ibn ʿArabī gives us one more kind of veridical dream in which there are no symbols. Here the imagination does not interfere. The heart reflects directly the spiritual impressions (*maʿāni ghaybiyya,* meanings from the unknowable) before the imagination can read into them any symbolic meaning. Dreams of this kind need no interpretation. They are revelations of the Real itself, and they correspond in every detail to things seen (later) in the external world. To this class of dreams belong some kinds of *wahy* (revelations) and *ilhām* (inspiration), which spring directly from the individual soul.

Gnostics create by means of a mysterious power that Ibn ʿArabī calls *al-himma* (spiritual will), which can produce changes and create objects in the external world wherever it is concentrated.

To understand what he means by *khayāl* it is necessary first to understand what he calls the *ḥaḍarāt-i khamsa* (the Five Presences) of the Divine devolution. The *ḥaḍrat al-shuhūd* (the Presence of Witnessing and of the Senses) is regarded as the devolvement of the higher Presence of Similitudes (*ḥaḍrat al-mithāl*), which is often referred to as the Presence of Angels (*ḥaḍrat al-malakūt*); which is a devolvement of the Presence of Compelling (*ḥaḍrat al-jabarūt*); which is a devolvement of the Presence of the Unknowable (*ḥaḍrat al-ghayb*). The fifth *ḥaḍra* is that of the Perfect Man, which englobes all the others.

Once the meaning of these *ḥaḍarāt* is grasped, many obscure points of Ibn ʿArabī's theory become more intelligible. **Nothing is really created anew either by God or Man, but things may be said to be preserved by God in one or other of these planes of the Five Presences.**

Creating, therefore, in the sense of preserving what already exists in one or other or all of these *ḥaḍarāt*, may be attributed to Man. The heart of Man (the Perfect Man) is a centre for all the divine activities. It reflects, like a mirror, all the forms in which Reality reveals Itself. By concentrating on the form of anything in one or more of these *ḥaḍarāt* by means of the *himma* (which is a power of the heart), the mystic has a perfect control over that thing, and through this control the thing is preserved in one *ḥaḍra* or another so long as the concentration of the *himma* is maintained.

The difference between the creation of God and that of Man (the Perfect Man), on this theory, is that God's 'creations' are preserved at all times and in all the *ḥaḍras*, because God never becomes forgetful of His creations; while those of Man are preserved only at one time or other, and in one *ḥaḍra* or other, and never in all the *ḥaḍarāt*. As soon as Man becomes forgetful of his creations, they disappear – not from existence altogether, for nothing disappears from existence, but from the *ḥaḍarāt* of which Man has become forgetful. It is not like recalling mental images and preserving them in a mind: it is 'preserving' what has existence outside the place of the *himma*. Ibn 'Arabī says that although the gnostic possesses this mysterious power called *himma*, and is able to dispense it (*taṣarruf*), a true gnostic would refrain from exercising it for two reasons:

a. He realises his state as a mere servant (*'abd*) of God and therefore he prefers to leave creation to his Lord.

b. He knows that the dispenser and dispensee are essentially one. Ibn 'Arabī mentions the two Shaykhs, Abū-l Su'ūd Ibn Shibl and Abū Madyan, as belonging to this class of mystics who abandoned *taṣarruf* in disdain. But a Sufi may exercise his *taṣarruf*, Ibn 'Arabī adds, if God bids him to do so. This was the case with 'Abd al-Qādir al-Gīlānī.

Fanā' & Baqā'

The mystic does not become God, for there is no becoming: he is essentially one with God in the sense that everything else is. What the mystic knows, he experiences here. The divine is already there: it is you – not even an element, as Ḥallāj calls it, in your nature, but an aspect. Ibn 'Arabī himself repudiates the idea that a mystic passes away from his own 'self', or becomes God. He cannot be contemptuous enough of people who make such assertions.

According to Ibn 'Arabī, *fanā'* may mean either of two things:

a. *Fanā'* in a mystical sense, by which he means the 'passing away' of ignorance, and the 'remaining' (*baqā'*) of infallible knowledge (gained by intuition) of the essential oneness of the Whole. The mystic does not pass away from his 'self', but he realises its essential non-existence as a form.

b. *Fanā'* in a metaphysical sense, by which he means the 'passing away' of the forms of the phenomenal world, and the continuance of the One Universal Substance. This is, as Mr. Winfield puts it, the eternal process of "phenomena being constantly annihilated in the Universal Noumenon": the new creation (*al-khalq al-jadīd*) explained before. It is summed up by Ibn 'Arabī's own words; "The disappearance of a form is its *fanā'* at the moment of the manifestation (*tajallī*) of God in another form".

The mystical *fanā'*, he says, is imperfect. The mystic realises that he, as a form, has no existence *per se*, but, owing to the very nature of the form, he cannot completely pass away from it. How can it be possible even for a mystic, he asks, to die to 'self' and be at the same time conscious of God as the all-embracing Reality? Consciousness itself means persistence of 'self'.

Ibn 'Arabī makes a fundamental distinction between two mystical states which, he believes, have been confused by other mystics:

1. The passing away from all traces and characteristics of 'self' or personality. This state is similar to sleep. "The mystic is neither with his 'self' nor with his Lord; he is asleep, he is ignorant."

2. The passing away of 'self' in a state of intuitive knowledge in which the essential unity of the Whole is revealed. This is the aspect of the mystical experience which Ibn 'Arabī emphasises. It is knowledge of an infallible nature that Ibn 'Arabī is after. To say that I have become God, or died to 'self' in any real sense, is ignorance; and to see your 'self' alone in a mystical experience is polytheism. The perfect mystic, therefore, is one who sees God and 'self' in the mystical experience, both by mystical knowledge and feeling, i.e. the perfect mystic is the one who recognises both Essence and form, but realises their essential unity and the absolute non-existence of the form.

The particular soul which contemplates the One as itself, or in itself, never left the One.

According to Ibn 'Arabī, *fanā'* is a gradual process of various stages (one does not go through each necessarily) in which the mystic knows by intuition (*dhawq* – taste) his real place in relation to God.

Some of these stages are as follows:

1. The passing away from all actions whatever. In this stage the mystic realises that God alone is the absolute and the only agent in the universe. The real agent is God Himself.
2. Passing away from one's own personality (*dhāt*), by which he means that the mystic realises in such a state the non-existence of his phenomenal 'self' and the subsistence (*baqā'*) of the unchangeable, unperishable substance which is its essence.
3. Passing away from the whole world, i.e. the cessation of contemplating the phenomenal aspect of the world, and the realisation of the real aspect which underlies the phenomena.
4. Passing away from all that is 'other than God', even from the very act of passing away. One of the conditions of this stage is that the mystic must cease to be conscious of himself as a contemplator. It is God Himself that contemplates and is contemplated. He is seen in every one of His infinite 'states' (*shu'ūn*) i.e. manifestations.
5. The passing away from all the attributes of God and their 'relations', i.e. the contemplation of God as the Essence of the universe rather than the 'cause' of it, as the philosophers say. The mystic then does not regard the universe as an effect of a cause, but as 'Reality in Appearance' (*ḥaqq fī ẓuhūr*). He realises the meaninglessness of causality and such Divine Names as the Creator, the Designer, the Giver and so on. This last stage is the ultimate goal, and is

what Ibn 'Arabī calls the station of absolute transcendence of the unity.

In every one of the so-called mystical stages of *fanā'*, the essential unity of being is realised by the mystic. To every stage of *fanā'* corresponds a stage of *baqā'* (subsistence): that which passes away is the phenomenal and that which endures is the Real. The ultimate goal of Ibn 'Arabī's mysticism is the attainment of what he calls 'true knowledge'.

Fanā' and *baqā'* are two complementary aspects of one and the same experience, in which the Real is 'seen' to persist, the phenomenal to pass away. *Fanā'* is characteristic of all that is 'other than God'; *baqā'* of God alone. In every one of these stages one of the 'veils' – i.e. the characteristics of the so-called phenomenal world as we know it; all that is called other than God – is removed, and the mystic is brought one step nearer to the Truth. When all the 'veils' are lifted up, Reality appears in its absolute nakedness, and absolute freedom of the soul is reached. The mystic is then said to have arrived (*waṣala*) at his goal, where lies his happiness. This goal is not God, for how can it be God, Ibn 'Arabī says, when He is the very one that arrived at the goal?

The supreme happiness of the mystic is in realising, by means of mystic intuition, his essential unity with God. What was for him knowledge of certainty (*'ilm al-yaqīn*) is now the very 'eye' or vision of certainty (*'ayn al-yaqīn*); and when he transcends the stage of the duality of the knower and the known, he reaches the highest stage of mystical life in which he is face to face with the reality of certainty (*ḥaqq al-yaqīn*).

Beliefs

There are three ways in which beliefs regarding God are formed:

1. The way of the follower of a prophet
2. The way of the philosopher and free-thinker
3. The way of the gnostic (*al-ʿārif*)

The believer, or follower, fashions his beliefs after the manner of his prophet; the thinker bases his on reason; the gnostic – who may be said to have no definite belief like the other two – is guided by his immediate perception (*dhawq* – taste) of the Truth. Each of them has a conception in which he finds his God, "and each will, when the truth is revealed in the next world, recognise the object of his belief (i.e. his God) in the infinite Being who will then appear in all the forms of belief". Only then will they fully apprehend the meaning of their beliefs, when they obtain an immediate 'vision' of Reality as it really is. Only then shall we see for ourselves, with keenness of sight that will never be dimmed, the One object which reflects Itself on the infinite mirror of our beliefs, and know what the meaning of God's *huwiyya* (Essence) is. People who believe that God is limited to any particular form will recognise Him in that particular form and no other; and people like the Muʿtazilites, who believe in the fulfilment of His threat, will not recognise Him in His absolute Mercy which embraces all things; and so on. Only gnostics, Ibn ʿArabī says, will recognise Him in all the forms of belief in which He will reveal Himself, as they now recognise Him in all His manifestations; for the gnostics are the *hayūlā* of all beliefs.

The forms of belief in God vary according to the nature of the objects of those beliefs, but any belief which deprives God of His absolute universality, or falls short of explaining His full nature as being both a transcendent and an immanent Reality, is partial and imperfect. To worship a star or a tree is to worship a god who is but a partial manifestation of the Real God, but to worship Him in all forms is to worship *Allāh*, who is the only true object of worship. All other gods are 'intelligible objects of beliefs'. We create them in our minds. Everyone is right in his belief, no matter how partial it is, but wrong in asserting that the object of his belief is (when it is not) *Allāh*.

Gnostics alone worship the true God whose Name (*Allāh*) is the most universal of all the Divine Names. They are called 'Worshippers of Time' (*'ubbād al-waqt*), because they worship God at every moment of Time in a fresh manifestation. Their position is a peculiar one: they combine the belief of the philosopher, who asserts pure transcendence of God, with that of the polytheist, who asserts pure immanence; for neither transcendence alone nor immanence alone explains the full nature of Reality. Immanence alone leads to a form of polytheism which Ibn 'Arabī denounces, and transcendence alone leads to a duality of God and universe which Ibn 'Arabī rejects. The only religion left for him is the universal religion, which includes all religions and which is *Islām*. *Islām* is not only the religion of Muḥammad, but the embodiment of all religions and beliefs.

Ibn 'Arabī maintains that love is the basis of all forms of worship, and that the only true form of worship is Love. To worship is to love the object worshipped. But 'love' is a principle which pervades all beings and binds them together. It is one universal kind, although it appears to be a multiplicity in forms. It is an essential unity: the Divine Essence itself. Therefore the highest and the truest object of worship, the highest manifestation (*majlā*) in which God is worshipped, is love. **"I swear by the reality of Love that Love is the cause of all Love; were it not for Love (residing) in the heart, Love (God) would not be worshipped."**

People's beliefs are determined by, and vary according to, their own aptitude (*isti'dād*). This, Ibn 'Arabī says, is what Junayd meant by saying, "the colour of water is the colour of the vessel which contains it". The part that God plays in the matter is that of an Omniscient Being who knows from eternity what every individual belief is going to be, but even His knowledge is determined by the nature of the beliefs and that of the people to whom they belong. Commenting on the Qur'ānic verse, "Verily God is not unjust to His servants", Ibn ʿArabī says, "I (i.e. God) did not ordain polytheism which dooms them to misery, and then demand of them what lay not in their power to perform. No, I dealt with them only according as I knew them, and I knew them only by what they 'gave' me from themselves, of what they themselves really are. Hence if there is any wrong, they are the wrong-doers. I said to them nothing but what my Essence decreed that I should say to them, and my Essence is known to me as it is... It is mine to say and it is for them to obey or not to obey."

The ultimate goal is the realisation of the essential Unity of the One Reality which is the All, and the full recognition of the Principle of Love – for God is Love – which pervades and unites the Whole. In this 'religion' God is impersonal, but those who are incapable of conceiving Him as such may worship Him in any form they please, provided they know what the real object of their worship is. **To worship the Real God is to contemplate Him in everything, including yourself.**

Good & Evil

If we say we are responsible, we are right, and if we say God is responsible, we are equally right: but we must always remember the point of view. God does not will in the sense that He chooses, but in the sense that He decrees what He knows will take place. That the thing or action which God has decreed should take place depends entirely on its own necessary laws. Logically, Ibn ʿArabī argues, a 'possible' thing or action may be one or other of many alternative things or actions, but actually it is only one: the one God knows will take place. It is impossible for God to will what lies not in the nature of things. The intrinsic laws of Man are the deciding factor in all that he does, good or evil.

Evil, for Ibn ʿArabī, **is not a positive quantity**. Pure evil is the same as pure not-being and pure darkness, and pure good is pure being and pure light. According to him and Suhrawardī al-Muqtūl, the difference between 'light' and 'darkness' is not one of contrariety, but one of existence and non-existence. Ibn ʿArabī, for example, includes such things as physical pain, failing health, animal cruelty, and so on, in what he calls evil. For him, all evil, ethical or otherwise, is relative. There is nothing that is evil in itself, and God never creates any evil. Things and actions are called evil for one or other of the following reasons:

1. Because one religion or other regards them as such;
2. Relative to a certain ethical principle or customary standard approved by a community;
3. Because they are incongruous with some individual temperament;
4. Because they fail to satisfy some natural, moral or intellectual desires of an individual; and so on.

Apart from these and other similar standards by which we measure the goodness or evilness of things or actions, there is nothing, Ibn ʿArabī says, except the bare essence of things (*aʿyān al-mawjūdāt*) which we cannot describe as good or evil.

In addition to things which have already been mentioned as coming under Ibn ʿArabī's category of evil, we may include ignorance, falsehood, disharmony, disorder, sin, infidelity, incompatibility of temper and so on. In all these things there is something lacking; some positive being or quality which, if added to the things or actions we call evil, would convert them into good. Nothing is evil: all that **is**, is good. In other words, what we call evil is subjective, not an objective reality.

But even good as contrasted with evil is subjective and relative. The only good that is absolute is Pure Being (God, the Good).

Our judgement of the goodness and evilness of things is relative to our knowledge. We call a thing or an action evil because of our ignorance of the good that is hidden therein. "Everything", he says, "has an external and an internal aspect. In its internal aspect lies the purpose of the Creator, and if we are ignorant of such purpose, we are apt to pronounce such a thing to be evil".

Ibn ʿArabī gives medicine as an illustration of what he wishes to say. Here is a case of an apparent evil (e.g. the unpleasantness resulting from tasting a repugnant medicine) and of a positive good of which the patient, who condemns his medicine as evil, may be ignorant. A thing like medicine, therefore, is regarded as evil for two reasons, and it is a relative evil in each case:

1. It lacks some positive qualities, on account of the absence of which it does not appeal to the taste of the patient, who regards it as evil;
2. It is considered an evil relative to the knowledge of the patient, who is ignorant of the good that is in it.

In itself medicine cannot be described as good or evil, and the same may be said of all other goods and evils. Ibn ʿArabī adds that ultimately both good and evil come from God. To put it in other words, all things are manifestations of God and all actions are His actions, only we call some of them good and others bad. The Mercy of God is shown in all things and actions, for it is through His Mercy that everything has come to being.

Ibn ʿArabī makes a distinction between two kinds of Divine Will:

1. The *mashīʾa*, by which he means something like the Divine Consciousness which is present in all things: the

eternal Power of God which decrees that things (potential or actual) should be what they are. Ibn ʿArabī means by *mashī'a* the Divine Essence Itself. He calls it *al-wujūd* (Being or God) and approves of Abu Tālib al-Makkī's calling it *al-ʿarsh al-dhāt* (the throne of the Essence).

2. The creative Will (*irāda*), by which he means a power by means of which God brings into external manifestation potential existents.

"Sin is disobedience, not to the Divine Will, not to the creative command of God (*al-amr al-takwīnī*), but to mediate religious command (*al-amr bi-l-wāsita*, or *al-amr al-taklīfī*)." In Ibn ʿArabī's view, also that of Ḥallāj, this Divine Command (*amr*) is not a real command (*amr*) but is what they call *ibtilā'* (trial). It would have been against God's wisdom if He had not created things which we call evil, or decreed actions which we call sins. The world would not have been complete or perfect, for it is a part of the perfection of the world to include what we call imperfection. God's complete perfections would not have been manifested; the manifested world is the relative world and in a relative state 'the more' or 'the less' are of the nature of the relative state. He also adds that we are enjoined to accept not that which God has decreed (*al-maqḍī bihi*), but the Decree itself (*al-qaḍā'*). "Prayer for removal of evil should be submitted to God", Ibn ʿArabī says; "...it behoves a person in pain to pray to God to remove it, because by so doing God removes it from Himself". On the contrary, Ibn ʿArabī argues, to try to refrain from complaint to God when you are afflicted with pain is to defy Fate, and this is ignorance.

This, in outline, is Ibn ʿArabī's Ethics. The pivot round which it all turns is self-realisation. Every thing and every action has one ultimate aim which it is bound to achieve, and this is to realise itself; and in so doing it realises one or other of God's infinite perfections, which include the so-called imperfections according to Ethics or Religion.

His descriptions of Heaven and Hell are merely "allegorical representations of states" and "corporealisations of ideas". "What we learn from tradition", he says, "is mere words, and it is left to us to find out what such words mean." Paradise, he says, comes from the verb *janna*, to conceal, and the *janna* of all is the Divine Essence in which all multiplicity will be 'concealed'. On the other hand, Hell (*jahannam*) means distance or farness (*bu'd*), and the real hell lies in imagining that there is a real chasm between you and God and not realising your essential oneness with Him.

The 'Day of Grief' (*yawm al-ḥasra*) he understands as the 'Day of Unveiling', from *ḥasara*, to unveil; i.e. the day on which the One Essence will be revealed in Its absolute universality. Heaven and Hell are two subjective states. Hell is selfhood. Heaven, on the other hand, is the realisation of the divine aspect of his being. Of life after death Ibn 'Arabī has no doubt whatever, for life, according to him, is continuous and unceasing. There is only One Being in existence and there is therefore but one life. "Though the damned", Ibn 'Arabī says, "will enter the abode of misery, they will experience therein happiness which will be different from that of Paradise." The only kind of torment the damned will experience is a negative one; they will be deprived, for a time, of the greatest happiness of all, i.e. the realisation of their inseparable unity with God. The One whence all things come is the One to which they will all return. When we return to the One, we will realise the truth or falsity of our beliefs, and our position relative to Him will be determined entirely by the nature of such beliefs. The gnostics alone will be in immediate contact with Him, and this will constitute the highest happiness in Heaven. Souls in the spiritual world will be an essential unity, yet preserving a degree of consciousness that will enable them to enjoy their various grades of spiritual happiness.

Love & Beauty

The One is the all-embracing Being – the ultimate ground of all existence. It is identified with the all-active and the all-willing Principle. It is the all-pervading Consciousness; the same Reality as the all-prevailing Love and Beauty.

The fundamental factor underlying all these manifestations of the One Reality is, according to Ibn ʿArabī, Divine Love. He recognises three kinds of Love: natural love, spiritual love and Divine Love. The first two are species of the third. Divine Love means the essential Love of the One – the eternal love which is the source of all other kinds. Before any form of modalisation, the One, in His supreme isolation and simplicity, loved Himself for and in Himself, and loved to be known and to be manifested. This was the cause of creation. In loving Himself, the One loved all the *aʿyān* of things latent in His Essence, and hence they are impregnated with love that they now manifest in different ways. "The love of the *aʿyān* began", Ibn ʿArabī says, "when they were still in the Blindness (*al-ʿamā*), when they first heard God's creative word (Be)."

Spiritual love means mystical love, of which the ultimate aim is realisation of the essential unity of the lover and the Beloved. Divine Love, in refinding itself, realises its affinity as a 'form' with the Universal Love of the Whole. This is the most perfect kind of love. It is the love of the Whole as a Whole (as an Essence) and as a part (as a particular mode of the Essence). It is what the Sufis mean by rapture (*hayamān*). Ibn ʿArabī says that the ultimate goal of love is to know the reality of love and that the reality of love is identical with God's Essence. Love is not an abstract quality superadded to the Essence. It is not a relation between a lover and an object loved. This is the true love of the gnostics, who know no particular object of love. It is the profane that love forms. Nothing is loved except God, just as nothing is worshipped except Him. When we say that we love x, y or z, what we really mean is that we love God in the form of x, y or z; and it is ignorance to say that we love x, y or z themselves, just as it is ignorance to say that we worship x, y or z themselves. When we say we love God, or anything, we mean that God loves Himself in us or in any other form.

The third kind of love is natural love, the object of which is self-satisfaction, regardless of the object loved. In spiritual love, the 'self' and all its desires are sacrificed in the interest of the Beloved. In natural love the object is sacrificed. Ibn ʿArabī includes under natural love what he calls elemental love *(al-ḥubb al-ʿunṣurī)*, under which all physical, psychological, and even mechanical attractions can be classed. Even this he regards as a manifestation of the Divine Love in its lowest and crudest form.

According to Ibn ʿArabī, love is not an end in itself; it has no intrinsic value. **The basis and cause of all love is Beauty.** We love God because God is Beautiful, and He loves us and all His creation because He loves the Beautiful. God's Beauty is the source of all types of Beauty. It is the source of all spiritual and intellectual beauty as well as beauty of form, although in itself God's Beauty is above all form and shape. God loves beauty of form because form reflects His own Beauty, as it reflects His Being. In abstract beauty as well as in beauty of form, therefore, God ought to be loved and worshipped, and this is how a perfect Gnostic knows Him, loves Him and worships Him.

Love is the cause of creation (or self-manifestation of the One in His infinite Forms), but it is also the cause of the return of all the manifestations to the One. "Does not God say," Ibn ʿArabī asks, "O David, My yearning for them is greater than their yearning for Me?" Love is the working principle in all manifestations of the One, from the highest to the lowest. It reaches its zenith in Man, the Perfect Man, who above all creation experiences all the three kinds of Love. Through Love, the Whole is bound together and through it the object of creation is realised. Thus the whole system is perfectly complete.

Index of Names & Arabic terms

A

ʿabd 60
ʿabd al-kāmil 36
ʿAbd al-Qādir al-Gīlānī 41, 60
Abū Madyan 60
Abu Saʿid al-Kharrāz 23
Abu Tālib al-Makkī 69
Abū-l Suʿūd Ibn Shibl 60
Adam 36, 42
ʿadam al-maḥḍ 10
Affifi, A.E. 5
afrād 41
Aḥad 24
aḥadiyya 16, 24, 32
aḥbāb 41
aḥkām 9, 12, 13, 19, 30
ʿālam 10
ʿālam al-amr 53
ʿālam al-arwāḥ 29
Allāh 25, 65
ʿamā 24, 32, 56, 71
amīr 53
amr 69
amr al-taklīfī 69
amr al-takwīnī 69
amr bi-l-wāsita 69
Anā'l-Ḥaqq 50
ʿaql 54
ʿaql al-kulli 52
ʿarad 53
ard 45
ʿārif 11, 64
ʿarsh 38
ʿarsh al-dhāt 69
arwāh 57
Ashʿarites 18

'awālim 10
awhām 48
a'yān 26, 27, 28, 30, 36, 71
a'yān al-mawjūdāt 67
a'yān al-thābita 25, 26, 27, 29, 34
'ayn 12, 27, 36
'ayn al-basīra 57
'ayn al-baṣīra 49
'ayn al-yaqīn 63

B

baqā' 60, 62, 63
barzakh 38, 40
Bayazid 31, 36
bayt al-ma'mūr 38
bu'd 70

D

dhāt 62
dhawq 45, 48, 62, 64
ḍidd 24

F

fanā' 39, 47, 61, 62, 63
farq 12
fayḍ al-ilāhī 46
Fuṣūṣ al-Ḥikam 5
Futūḥāt al-Makkīya 27

G

Gabriel 51, 56
ghayb 16, 45
Ghazālī 57

H

habā 40
ḥaḍarāt 24, 51, 59
ḥaḍarāt-i khamsa 59

ḥādith 20
ḥaḍra 51, 59
ḥaḍrat al-asmā' 29
ḥaḍrat al-dhātiyya 57
ḥaḍrat al-ghayb 59
ḥaḍrat al-ilāhiyya 25
ḥaḍrat al-jabarūt 59
ḥaḍrat al-khayāl 56
ḥaḍrat al-malakūt 59
ḥaḍrat al-mithāl 59
ḥaḍrat al-raḥmāniyya 29
ḥaḍrat al-shuhūd 59
ḥakam 44
Ḥallāj 45, 50, 60, 69
ḥaqā'iq 34
ḥaqīqa 21
ḥaqīqat al-ḥaqā'iq 32, 34, 40
ḥaqq 11, 12, 13, 14, 15, 16, 37
ḥaqq al-mūṭlaq 9
ḥaqq al-yaqīn 63
ḥaqq fī ẓuhūr 62
hayamān 71
hayūlā 32, 33, 64
himma 58, 59, 60
ḥubb al-'unṣurī 72
ḥukm 27, 30
ḥulūl 14
huwiyya 26, 47, 64

I

Ibn Farīḍ 56
Ibn Rushd (Averroes) 19
ibtila 69
ilhām 58
'ilm al-ahwāl 45
'ilm al-'aql 45
'ilm al-asrār 45
'ilm al-ghayb 45
'ilm al-yaqīn 63

ʻilm ladunnī 45
imām 40
inā' 13
insān al-hayawānī 36
insān al-kabīr 36
insānu ʻayn al-ḥaqq 40
irāda 55, 69
Islām 42, 65
istafād al-wujūd 28
istiʻdād 65
iṭlāq 14, 16

J

jahannam 70
jamʻ 12
jamʻiyya al-ilāhiyya 37
Jāmī 48
janāb al-ilāhī 37
janna 70
Jīlī 37
jism al-kulli 32
Junayd 65

K

Kaʻba 38
kalima 40
kashf 46
kawn al-jāmiʻ 35
kawn jāmiʻ 36
khalīfa 35, 40, 42
khalq 11, 12, 13, 14, 15, 37
khalq al-jadīd 61
khalwa 30
khayāl 56, 59
khayālāt 57
kitāb 33
kitāb al-masūr 32
kufr 14

M

ma'āni 57
ma'āni ghaybiyya 58
mafātīḥ al-awwal 29
mafātīḥ al-ghayb 29
māhiyya 26
māhiyyāt 9
majlā 65
mansūb ilayhi 55
maqḍī bihi 69
maraḍ 55
marātib 10, 21
ma'rifa 41
martaba al-ilāhiyya 32
mashī'a 68
mithl 24
mudrik 47
Muḥammad 35, 37, 40, 41, 42, 56, 65
mulqī 51
munfaṣil 56
muqtaḍayāt 27
Mu'tazilites 64
muttaṣil 57
Muwaḥḥid 15

N

nūr 53
nafs al-kulliya 52
nisab 50
nisba 55
nisba al-shakhṣiyya 55
nisba muṭlaqa 55
nubuwwa 41

P

Philo of Alexandria 40
Plotinus 29, 34, 48, 51

Q

qaḍā' 69
qābil 29
qalām al-ā'lā 33
Qur'ān 51
qutb 40

R

Rabb 24
risāla 41
ru'yā al-ṣādiqa 57
rubūbiyya 32
Rūḥ 28, 40, 50

S

shāfi' 40
shahwa 55
sharā'i' 42
sharṭ 18
shuhūd 47
shu'ūn 62
ṣifāt al-tanzīh 16, 23
ṣifāt al-tashbīh 23
Spinoza 45
ṣūra 35
subuḥāt al muḥriqa 24
Suhrawardī al-Muqtūl 67
sūrat al-ḥaqq 40

T

ta'alluq 25
ta'ayyun al-awwal 26, 29, 40
taḥaqquq 25
tajallī 31, 48, 61
tajalliyāt 31, 32
takhalluq 25
takhayyul 57
takwīn 19

tanzīh 14
tanzīh al-tawḥīd 16
taqyīd 14, 16
taṣarruf 60
tashbīh 14
tawḥīd 15, 30
thubūt 19, 46
thumma 19
ṭūl 45

U

'ubbād al-waqt 65
umanā' 41

W

wāḥidiyya 24
wahy 58
wajh 21
wājib al-wujūd 9, 11
walī 41
waratha 41
waṣala 63
wilāya 41, 42
wujūd al-kulli 9
wujūd al-mutlaq 9

Y

yawm al-ḥasra 70

Z

ẓuhūr 19